The AMAZING PHOTODELUXE™ Book

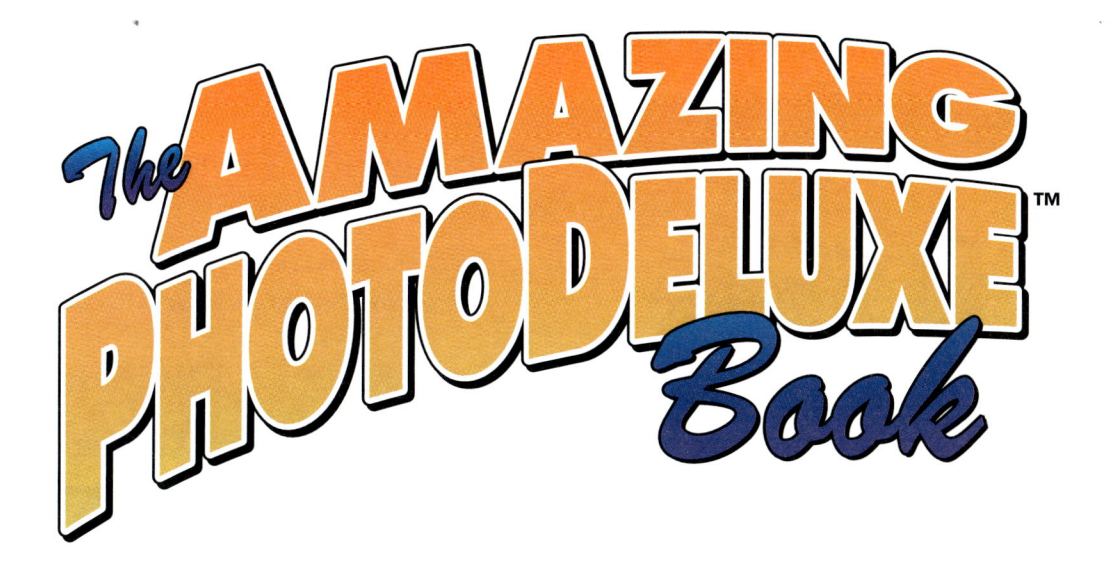

Adobe Press
Mountain View, California

Ten Golden Rules of Learning Adobe PhotoDeluxe

1 Have Fun!

2 Try out the Guided Activities first.

3 Make sure the Adobe PhotoDeluxe CD is in your CD-ROM drive and mounted on the desktop before you try to use photos from the Decorate, Samples, or Template folders.

4 Click Main on the opening screen to get to the On Your Own area (you must be working in On Your Own to use this book).

5 To save hours of frustration, read Sections 1 and 2 of this book before you try out the techniques.

6 Choose Help from the Apple menu to get information on specific tools, commands, or topics.

7 You can turn off Clue Cards by choosing File>Preferences>Turn Off All Clue Cards.

8 The more internal memory you have, the better Adobe PhotoDeluxe runs.

9 The more available hard disk storage you have, the happier you'll be.

10 You can't save to a CD-ROM.

Contents

1 Welcome to Adobe PhotoDeluxe   1

How to use this book, how digital images are displayed, how to convert your photos into digital images

2 Become an Instant Expert   11

Fundamental concepts and skills—opening photos, making selections, working with tools, selecting colors, using layers

3 Everyday Uses   31

Twenty Adobe PhotoDeluxe techniques to solve your most common photo problems

4 Special Effects   125

Twenty Adobe PhotoDeluxe techniques to expand your horizons

5 Save, Print, and Store Photos   223

Sharing your photos in print, via e-mail, and on the Internet; archiving and retrieving your photos

Index   237

Copyright © 1996 Adobe Systems Incorporated. All rights reserved.

No part of this publication may be reproduced, stored in a retrieval system, or transmitted, in any form or by any means, electronic, mechanical, photocopying, recording, or otherwise, without the prior written permission of Adobe Systems Incorporated.

Library of Congress Catalog No.: 95-81209

ISBN: 1-56830-266-5

10 9 8 7 6 5 4 3 2   First Printing: April 1996

The information in this book is furnished for informational use only, is subject to change without notice, and should not be construed as a commitment by Adobe Systems Incorporated. Adobe Systems Incorporated assumes no responsibility for any errors or inaccuracies that may appear in this book. The software mentioned in this book is furnished under license and may only be used or copied in accordance with the terms of such license.

Adobe, the Adobe Press logo, Acrobat, Adobe Fetch, Adobe Illustrator, Adobe PageMaker, Adobe PhotoDeluxe, and Adobe Photoshop and are trademarks of Adobe Systems Incorporated. All other brand or product names are the trademarks or registered trademarks of their respective holders.

Printed in the United States of America by Shepard Poorman Communications Corporation, Indianapolis, Indiana. Published simultaneously in Canada.

Adobe Press books are published and distributed by Macmillan Computer Publishing USA. For individual, educational, corporate, or retail sales accounts, call 1-800-428-5331, or 317-581-3500. For information address Macmillan Computer Publishing USA, 201 West 103rd Street, Indianapolis, IN 46290.

SECTION 1

Welcome to Adobe PhotoDeluxe

You're about to enter an amazing world. If this is your first experience with computer pictures, prepare to be delighted. If you've already discovered the fascination of creating and altering digital images, prepare to be awed by the simplicity and power of Adobe PhotoDeluxe™.

This book assumes that you're familiar with your computer and know how to use the mouse, click buttons, choose commands from menus, and select options from dialog boxes. If you need more practice with any of these skills, see the documentation that came with your computer.

Working with images 2

How to use this book 2

About digital photos 4

Getting photos into Adobe PhotoDeluxe 5

Don't violate that copyright! 8

Working with images

If you've used word-processing, layout, or drawing programs, you've probably had some experience using pictures on your computer. In that case, you know that adding pictures to a file makes the file bigger and slows down scrolling and printing. Because Adobe PhotoDeluxe deals exclusively in images, you'll find that your Adobe PhotoDeluxe files are larger than the ones you're used to working with. In addition to requiring more space, graphic images also require more memory. The more disk space and memory you have, the faster and more enjoyable it is to work in Adobe PhotoDeluxe. So, when your next birthday rolls around, ask for more memory and a gigabyte hard disk!

How to use this book

The Amazing Adobe PhotoDeluxe Book is an idea book, not a tutorial. The techniques are offered as suggestions and guides to help you produce specific effects as you work with your own images.

Adobe PhotoDeluxe has two areas—Guided Activities and On Your Own. The Guided Activities are structured procedures for touching up and transforming photos and for creating cards, calendars, and flyers. When you're working in Guided Activities, you're limited to the steps in the activity. You might want to try out a few of the Guided Activities to get a feel for Adobe PhotoDeluxe before wandering around in On Your Own. With On Your Own, you can use all of Adobe PhotoDeluxe's features in any order or combination you choose.

The Amazing Adobe PhotoDeluxe Book is meant to be used when you're working in On Your Own. The book is divided into five sections.

- Section 1, "Welcome to Adobe PhotoDeluxe," explains how to use the book, describes how digital images are displayed on your computer, and tells you how to convert your photos into digital images. You need to read through this section at least once to get your bearings.

Welcome to Adobe PhotoDeluxe   3

- Section 2, "Become an Instant Expert," introduces the fundamental concepts and skills you need to get the most out of Adobe PhotoDeluxe. You should read this section before trying the ideas in this book and then refer to it whenever you need reminders.

- Section 3, "Everyday Uses," contains techniques you can use all the time to solve common photographic flaws and enhance your photos.

- Section 4, "Special Effects," demonstrates the power and excitement of Adobe PhotoDeluxe. These techniques are a bit more complicated than the techniques in Section 3.

- Section 5, "Save, Print, and Store Photos," details the ways you can share your Adobe PhotoDeluxe images. It explains how to print photos, put them in a slide show, display and send them online, and use them in other applications.

The steps and illustrations included in each technique provide the information you need to apply the technique to your own photos. To avoid a lot of repetition, the techniques focus on a task or effect, rather than explaining every detail of each step used in a project. When you don't understand how to do something, refer back Section 2.

> **Friendly Warning:** Before you attempt any of the techniques, be sure to read Section 2. You need to understand the concepts explained in this section in order to follow the book's techniques. You can save yourself hours of frustration by taking the time to read this section **first**.

This book does not replace the documentation that comes with Adobe PhotoDeluxe. It doesn't cover all of Adobe PhotoDeluxe's features, commands, and tools. When you need detailed information, refer to the *Adobe PhotoDeluxe User Guide* or to Adobe PhotoDeluxe's online help.

Adobe PhotoDeluxe also contains a set of built-in Clue Cards. These cards appear each time you click a button or select a tool. Once you've gotten comfortable with Adobe PhotoDeluxe, you might want to turn these cards off. To turn off the card for a specific button or tool, click the option in the individual card. To turn off the display of all Clue Cards, choose File>Preferences> Turn Off All Clue Cards.

About digital photos

To work in Adobe PhotoDeluxe you need digital images. When you digitize a photo, you convert a printed photograph or slide into information that your computer can understand. One way to digitize a photo is to use a scanner. The scanner passes light over the photo and changes the visual information into numerical information that tells the computer how dark and light each part of the photo should be and also how to display the color in the photo.

A digitized image is made up of **pixels** (picture elements). Think of pixels as similar to the tiles that make up a mosaic: individually they are small squares, but when viewed as a whole they make up a pattern or picture.

When viewed normally, pixels blend into a pattern

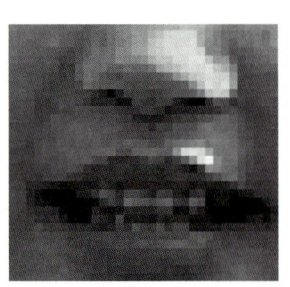

When magnified, pixels appear as individual squares

The number of pixels per inch (ppi) determines the image **resolution.** More pixels per inch produce higher resolutions which increases image quality. You set the resolution when you scan the photograph or slide.

Resolution = 72 ppi

Resolution = 144 ppi

Higher resolutions also increase file size. One square inch in an image with a resolution of 72 ppi contains 5,184 pixels. The same inch in an image with a resolution of 144 ppi contains 20,736 pixels! The file size grows from 96k to 256k.

When setting a resolution, you want to find the best compromise between image quality and file size.

Resolution = 72 ppi
File size = 96k

Resolution = 144 ppi
File size = 256k

Getting photos into Adobe PhotoDeluxe

There are several ways you can get your photos into digital form. You can scan the photos, have a service center scan them for you, take pictures with a digital camera, have your photos put on a CD or floppy disk, or buy any of the many collections of digital art available on CD-ROM.

Scanning

You can use any desktop scanner to scan the photos you want to use in Adobe PhotoDeluxe. You can scan using your scanner software or you can open Adobe PhotoDeluxe and scan from inside the program. As long as you have the driver for your scanner installed, you can scan the image and have it appear in an Adobe PhotoDeluxe window, all in one simple step. For information on installing scanner drivers and using the Scan Photo button and the Acquire command, see the Adobe PhotoDeluxe documentation.

If you don't own a scanner, you can take your photos to a copy center or service bureau and ask them to scan the photos for you. Here's what you need to tell the person at the center:

- What kind of computer you have (Macintosh or Windows)
- The resolution you want the image scanned at (see the following table)
- The type of file you want back (TIFF is a good choice because it works in lots of programs)
- The kind of storage device you want (floppy disk, removable cartridge, or CD-ROM)

The scan resolution you choose depends on how you're going to display the final photo. The following table recommends resolutions for common uses. If you think you might want to use the image in several ways, for example as a printed image and as a slide in an online screen show, scan at the higher resolution. You can always reduce the resolution in Adobe PhotoDeluxe, but the quality of the photo suffers if you increase the resolution in the program.

Scanning at a resolution higher than the recommended ppi doesn't increase the quality of your image because the computer or printer can't use the extra information. To keep the file size down (which speeds up the operation of Adobe PhotoDeluxe), use only as much resolution as you need for your output.

For the best output on	Use this resolution
Macintosh monitor	72 pixels per inch (ppi)
PC monitor	96 ppi
300 dpi laser printer	100 ppi
600 dpi laser printer	150 ppi
725 dpi inkjet printer	150 ppi
1200 dpi or higher image setter	1.5 times the screen frequency (lpi)*

* Talk to your service bureau for information about producing this very high-quality output.

Digital cameras

A digital camera doesn't use film; instead it uses sensors to capture the photos directly into digital format. Your photos are stored in the camera's built-in memory. When the memory is full, you can use Adobe PhotoDeluxe to download the pictures, or you can download them to your hard disk using the camera's software. After downloading, erase the camera's memory and you're ready to begin taking your next batch of photos.

Photos taken with inexpensive digital cameras have only low to medium resolution, but they're wonderful alternatives to 35-mm cameras for taking family snapshots and travel photos. Adobe PhotoDeluxe accepts images from the Apple QuickTake™ camera and the Kodak Digital Camera 40. Other digital cameras have software that you can add to Adobe PhotoDeluxe to use that particular camera. See the Adobe PhotoDeluxe documentation for more information on using digital cameras with Adobe PhotoDeluxe.

Taking photos to use in Adobe PhotoDeluxe

Once you start playing in Adobe PhotoDeluxe you'll probably think of a million things to do with all those photos you have lying around in drawers or hiding out in closets. But as you become more experienced, there may come a time when you can't find just the perfect image you need to complete a special project. Here are a few things you should keep in mind when you're taking a photo to use in Adobe PhotoDeluxe.

- If you're photographing a person to put into another background, photograph the person against a solid-colored wall or cloth, and make sure that the hair and clothes stand out from the background color. Avoid shadows around the body. This makes it easier to select only the person to add to a photo already in Adobe PhotoDeluxe.

- Take several photos at the same distance with similar facial expressions. That way, if one photo doesn't work, you can copy and paste from the other photos.

- If you're photographing a person or object to use in a collage, think about the size and position of the other people or objects in the existing photos. It's easier to photograph the object or person in a compatible position (standing or sitting? facing left or right? at what distance?) than it is to resize or manipulate the images later in Adobe PhotoDeluxe.

- Unless you're going for a special effect, scan the new photo at the same resolution as the existing image or images. This keeps the photos in the same size ratio and gives you the image you expect when you combine the photos.

Photos stored on CD-ROM

Many photo processing centers offer you the option of receiving your 35-mm photos on a Kodak® PhotoCD® in addition to the usual prints and negatives. A Kodak PhotoCD contains five versions of your photo, in different resolutions. Multiple resolutions guarantee that you'll have the resolution you need, no matter how you choose to display the final photo. Unlike regular photographic prints, images stored on CD never lose their original quality and color, and they won't get scratched or torn. Scanning a roll of film when you have it processed is the most economical way to use PhotoCD. One Kodak PhotoCD holds several rolls of 36-exposure film.

You can also have photos that have already been developed, including black-and-white photos, transferred to a CD-ROM, either by Kodak or by other centers that offer this service. This is a convenient way to gather together the best of your photo collection and have it readily available for use in Adobe PhotoDeluxe. Ask at the copy center or service bureau where you have your photos scanned for more information about transferring photos to a CD-ROM.

Art collections on CD-ROM

As more and more people use digital images in their work and for fun, there is a growing demand for **stock photos**—images that have been sold to a distributor to be included in CD collections. When you buy the CD, you also buy the right to use the image. Images on these CD-ROMs include people, nature, history, fine art, borders, textures, business scenes, everyday objects, maps, space, food, and so on. Most of these images are in full color and come in low and high resolutions.

Clip art, which comes in both black and white and color, and on floppy disks or CD-ROM, consists of drawn images, often with a cartoon-like quality. Designers use this art in advertisements and brochures. You might find clip art useful for invitations, flyers, and calenders, or to add whimsical characters or objects to your photos. Repeating clip art along the edge of a photo or inside a shape can produce interesting patterns. Catalogs of clip art are available from computer retailers and mail-order catalogs.

Digital art is also available through some online services, such as the Kodak Picture Exchange. This is art that you pay for and license for a specific use, not art that you just decide to download (see the following section on copyrights). Buying art in this way can be expensive, depending on the size of the file and the speed of your modem; downloading a large image can take a long time.

Don't violate that copyright!

The ease with which digital images can be copied, manipulated, and distributed has raised a lot of questions about the personal use of copyrighted images. U.S. law is fairly clear: "A copyright gives the authors of literary, dramatic, musical, artistic, and other intellectual properties limited exclusive rights to reproduce the work, create derivative works based on the original, distribute copies of the work, and perform or display the work in public."

It's relatively clear what it means to reproduce the work, but many people are confused by what constitutes a **derivative** work. Does this mean that you can copy a piece of sky or grass if you don't show the main part of the photo? Does it mean that the piece you "borrow" must recognizable in your image in order to be a violation? Does it mean that you can use another's work as part of a collage? The answer to all these questions is NO. You are not allowed any unauthorized use of any part of a copyrighted image.

Another area of confusion in copyright law is the term **fair use.** Fair-use privilege allows, in certain cases, a limited amount of copying for the purpose of commentary, news reporting, teaching, scholarship, or research. In most cases, fair use does not apply to the personal work you produce in Adobe PhotoDeluxe.

You are allowed to use art that is in the **public domain.** This is generally work for which the copyright has expired. Depending on the circumstances, copyrights can last for 100 years or more, so a work usually has to be quite old to be in the public domain. Note that this does not necessarily apply to photographs of old art. While the painting, sketch, or sculpture may be ancient, the photograph that you're scanning may be copyrighted. Even if you take the picture yourself, the piece of art is probably owned by a museum or collector who also owns the right to limit access to the art.

Are people public property? While you may have heard that public personalities can be used to illustrate newspapers and magazines, these are done by professional publishing companies with established legal departments that can determine who is and who isn't a public personality. In terms of the original work you might do at home, work, or school with Adobe PhotoDeluxe, you probably need a photo release form from anybody in a picture that will be published outside your home usage.

When you buy collections of art to use in your work, check the license agreement. The license may permit some images to be used only once. Others permit unlimited use. There are countless variations in between, so read the license agreement carefully of any collections of photography, clip art, or art work you purchase.

This book is a case in point. It uses hundreds of images. Some of these images are from stock CD-ROM collections, the rights to which have been licensed. Other photos are the original work of the authors, the editors, or other book participants. All the contributors, as well as the people included in all these photos, have signed a release form granting either the stock CD vendor, or the authors, or Adobe Systems (Adobe Press is the publisher) the right to use their photos in a published work. In addition, Adobe Press has copyrighted this book and has formally announced its copyright on page vi at the beginning of this book. Nothing in this book can be reproduced without the express permission of the publisher.

This is an introduction to copyright issues. Don't rely on this discussion to determine whether or not use of an image will violate a copyright. When in doubt, don't use it.

For more information write to the Copyright Office, Information and Publication Section LM-455, Library of Congress, Washington DC 20559. Readers in countries other than the United States should check with their country's copyright offices. Each country has unique applications and laws governing copyright.

SECTION 2

Become an Instant Expert

Whether you want to restore an old photo, get rid of annoying wrinkles, combine photos into a collage, or apply a special effect, most Adobe PhotoDeluxe techniques use the same basic concepts and procedures. Once you've mastered these fundamentals, you're ready to apply these steps to your own photos, no matter what effect you want to achieve.

The information in this section provides a foundation for following the steps in the techniques presented in the rest of this book. The techniques themselves focus on a procedure, project, or effect and don't contain detailed instructions for each action in every step. For example, almost every technique begins with a selection. Once you've read this section and learned how to make a selection, you'll be able to do this step automatically.

Read through this section and become familiar with these basics before you try any of the Amazing Adobe PhotoDeluxe techniques. Once you're off and running, refer back to this section whenever you need a refresher on the basics.

Opening photos 12

Making selections 13

Working with tools 17

Selecting a color 18

Holding photos 19

Retrieving photos 19

Using layers 20

Changing the size and resolution of a photo 25

Changing the magnification of a photo 27

Using menus 27

Saving and printing photos 28

Working efficiently 29

Opening photos

When you're working in On Your Own (which you get to from the opening screen of Adobe PhotoDeluxe), you have six choices for opening a digital file. Click Get Photo and then click one of the following buttons.

Opens a file stored on your hard disk. Adobe PhotoDeluxe opens all files in its own format. If the file you open is in another format, it's opened as an untitled file. The original file is not changed. Click Find and enter the name to locate a file.

Opens a sample art file. These files are stored on the Adobe PhotoDeluxe CD-ROM. You must have the Adobe PhotoDeluxe CD-ROM in your drive to open one of these files. Click a category, then double-click to open a sample file.

Opens a decorations file. You need an open file to add a decoration. These files are stored on the Adobe PhotoDeluxe CD-ROM. You must have the Adobe PhotoDeluxe CD-ROM in your drive to open one of these files. Click a category, then double-click to open a decoration file.

Opens a file that's stored in your digital camera. You must drag the camera's plug-in module into the Acquire/Export folder in the Adobe PhotoDeluxe Plug-ins folder to have it appear in the camera list. Connect your camera to the computer and then open the file.

Opens your scanner software so you can scan a photo and have it appear in an Adobe PhotoDeluxe window. You must drag the scanner's plug-in module into the Acquire/Export folder in the Adobe PhotoDeluxe Plug-ins folder to have it appear in the scanner list. Choose your scanner from the list and then scan as usual.

Opens a file stored on a Kodak Photo CD. You must have the PhotoCD in your drive to open a file. Double-click a photo to open it.

> If your camera or scanner doesn't have a plug-in that is compatible with Adobe PhotoDeluxe (or Adobe Photoshop™), save the digital photo or the scan as a TIFF or PICT file and store it on your hard disk.

If your copy center returns your scanned files on a floppy disk, copy the files to your hard disk and open them using the Open File button.

Making selections

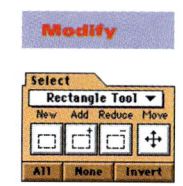

Adobe PhotoDeluxe tools and buttons affect an entire photo, unless you make a selection. You make selections by clicking a specific color or by using a tool to drag around an area in the photo. For example, if you want to change a background, you must select the background and delete it before you replace it.

To make a selection, open a file and click Modify. The Select palette appears on the left side of the Adobe PhotoDeluxe window. Choose a selection tool from the pop-up menu. The icons in the Select palette change to show the tool.

> Click the New button to begin the selection. Click the Add or Reduce button to modify a selection.

Select what you want to effect

Once you select an area you see the **selection border** around the selection (these dotted lines are sometimes called the **marquee** or **"marching ants"**). Everything outside of the selection border is protected from change. You can change colors, apply filters, or even delete, but only the area inside the dotted lines is affected by your actions.

Sky selected    Selection filled

Selecting an entire photo

To select an entire photo, click the All button on the Select palette. Unless you want to copy a photo, you don't need to select All because buttons and tools work on the entire photo if there's no selection.

Entire photo selected

Selecting standard shapes

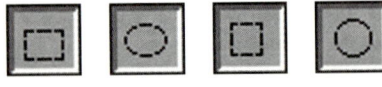

To select basic shapes, use the Rectangle, Oval, Square, or Circle tool. Choose the tool you want from the pop-up menu, click New, and then drag to select the shape.

When you're selecting shapes, it's sometimes easier to begin from the center. To start from the center, hold down the Option key as you drag. Release the Option key before releasing the mouse button.

Selecting from the edge    Selecting from the center

Selecting irregular shapes

To select irregular shapes, use the Polygon or Trace tool. To select an area using using straight lines, choose the Polygon tool from the pop-up menu, click to set the first point, move the cursor, and click again to set the next point. Double-click to close the polygon shape. To use the Trace tool, click and draw a freehand shape around the area you want to select.

Selecting irregular shapes    Tracing a selection

Selecting by color

You can select the areas in a photo that are a similar color. To select by color, choose the Color Wand tool from the pop-up menu and click a color in the photo. All the *adjacent* areas that are that same color are selected.

Selecting a color    All adjacent areas of the same color selected

Become an Instant Expert 15

To change how similar the colors must be to be selected, you can set the Color Wand **tolerance.** Choose File>Preferences> Cursors to set a new tolerance. Enter a higher value to select more colors with each click of the Color Wand. Enter a lower value to select fewer colors with each click. (This value stays the same until you change it, so if the Color Wand is selecting too much or too little, check the tolerance value.)

Tolerance = 20    Tolerance = 50

Adding to a selection

By clicking the New button, you start a new selection whenever you drag in your photo. To add to an existing selection, choose the selection tool you want to use and then click the Add button. Click the areas you want to add if you're using the Color Wand tool. Drag around the areas you want to add if you're using another tool and return the cursor to the starting point before releasing the mouse button.

Original selection

Selection increased

Reducing a selection

To reduce the area included in a selection, choose the selection tool you want to use and then click the Reduce button. Click the areas you want to delete if you're using the Color Wand. Drag around the areas you want to delete if you're using another tool and return the cursor to the starting point before releasing the mouse button.

Original selection    Selection decreased

Combining selection tools

When you're selecting irregular shapes, it's sometimes easier to begin with a shape tool or the Color Wand tool and select the larger areas first. Then use the Trace tool to fine tune the selection.

> Be sure the Add or Reduce button is selected when you're using multiple selection tools.

Shape selected using the Rectangle tool

Selection increased using the Trace tool

Inverting a selection

It's often easier to select the area you don't want selected and then invert the selection. For example, inverting is useful when you want to select an irregular shape that is surrounded by a solid color. Use the Color Wand tool to select the unwanted area and then click the Invert button to select everything that was not selected.

Background selected

Selection inverted

Deselecting a selection

To remove all selected areas from a photo, click the None button in the Select palette.

Background selected

Nothing selected

Moving or duplicating a selection

To move a selection, place the cursor inside the selection and drag the selection. To duplicate, rather than move, the selection, hold down the Option key as you drag.

Selection moved   Selection duplicated

Moving a selection border

If the selection is the right size and shape but in the wrong location, you can move just the selection border. To move the border, place the cursor in the selection border and then hold down the Option and Command keys as you drag.

Original selection   Selection border moved

Working with tools

Adobe PhotoDeluxe has five editing tools with which you can easily modify your selections—Brush, Color Change, Line, Eraser, and Smudge. You can also use the Brush and Line tools to draw on your photos.

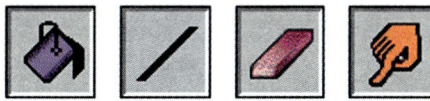

Selecting a brush

When you work with the Brush, Eraser, and Smudge tools, you select a brush size before you begin editing. Each tool has a Brushes palette that appears when you click the button.

The palette contains a row of hard-edges brushes and two rows of soft-edged brushes in varying sizes. The brushes in the bottom row are too large to show in the boxes, so the number underneath tells you the pixel width of the brush. Click to select the brush you want to use. See "Selecting a color" next, for information on choosing a painting color for these tools.

Drawing a line

You use the Line tool to draw straight lines of different widths. Click the button to show the Line tool options, then enter a number for the line width. See "Selecting a color" next, for information on choosing a painting color for the Line tool.

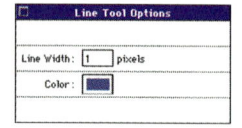

Tool shortcuts

Here are a couple of tips to help you when you're using these tools.

- To constrain a straight line to 45°, hold down the Shift key as you draw.

- To set an opacity for the tool, press a number key on the keyboard. Zero sets the opacity to 100%, 5 sets the opacity to 50%, 1 sets the opacity to 10%, and so on.

Selecting a color

When you're using the editing tools or when you're changing the color of a selection, you select the new color from the Color Swatches palette.

Click the color box in the palette or dialog box to show the Color Swatches palette. Click a swatch to select a new color. The new color appears in the color box and remains the painting or fill color until you select a new one.

Color before

Color after

If the color you want to use is not in the Color Swatches palette, you can select a color from the photo instead. Click the color box and then, with the Color Swatches palette open, click an area in the photo that's the color you want. The color you pick appears in the color box.

Color before

Color after

Holding photos

With Adobe PhotoDeluxe, you can have only one photo open at a time. When you want to combine photos, or use selections from several photos, you store the additional photos in the Hold Photo folder.

To store a photo, open it in Adobe PhotoDeluxe. If you want to use only part of the photo, select that part and delete the rest. Make any other editing changes and then click Save/Print>Save>Hold Photo. The photo disappears from the screen.

Retrieving photos

When you're ready to use the photo, click the triangle at the right edge of the Hold Photo button, below the Select palette. The contents of the Hold Photo folder appear. There are three ways to get a photo into the existing photo:

- Drag the photo over the open photo.
- Click to select the photo and then click Paste Layer.
- Double-click to select the photo and place it on top of the open photo at the same time.

When you use Paste Layer to place a photo, any layers in the photo are merged and the photo is pasted as a single layer.

Adobe PhotoDeluxe automatically creates a new layer when you bring in a photo from the Hold Photo folder. See "Using layers" next, for more information on layers.

To move the Hold Photo window, drag it by its title bar. To resize it, drag the resize box in the lower right corner. To remove a photo from the Hold Photo folder, select the photo and then click Delete.

Using layers

Layers are the secret weapon of Adobe PhotoDeluxe. Think of layers as sheets of clear plastic, stacked one on top of the other. Where there is nothing on a layer, you can see through it. When you add something to a layer, the filled space blocks the view of what's on the layers underneath.

By putting photos, or pieces of photos, on separate layers, you can move, resize, apply a special effect, change a color, change opacity, and blend the pieces together in any combination you like—all without affecting what's on the other layers.

In this example text is added on a separate layer above a background. You can try out different fonts and styles, resize the text, move the text to another location, or delete the text layer and try again, all without changing the background photo.

In this example the girl and the boy are on separate layers, above a background layer. You can now work with each layer individually. For example, you can duplicate the children, change the color of their clothes, or change their positions, and the background layer remains intact.

Or you can change the background layer to move them to exotic locations without changing their positions at all.

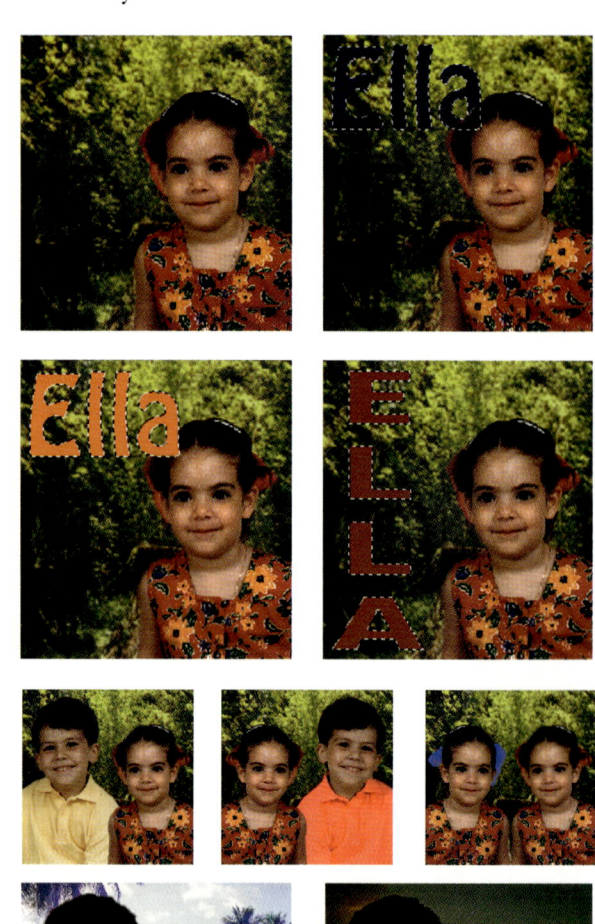

Adding layers

When you open a photo in Adobe PhotoDeluxe for the first time, it has one layer that appears in the Layers palette on the left side of the Adobe PhotoDeluxe window. When you open your own photo, it's called Layer 0; when you open a sample photo, this layer has a name or is called Layer 1.

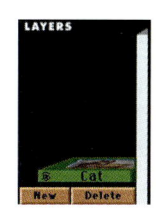

When you add text or a drop shadow to a photo, or add a photo that's stored in the Hold Photo folder, Adobe PhotoDeluxe automatically creates a new layer. To make your own layers, click the New button at the bottom of the Layers palette. The New Layer dialog box appears.

Enter a name for the layer.

Click OK to add the layer.

(You'll find out how to set the Opacity and Blend options in this dialog box as you work through the techniques in Sections 3 and 4.)

Each new layer appears on top of the existing layers in the Layers palette. When you add a new layer, it becomes the **active layer.** (The active layer is green.) Whatever you do—paint, fill, delete, or move—it affects only the active layer; all the other layers stay just as they were. To make a different layer the active layer, click it in the Layers palette.

You can have up to six layers in each Adobe PhotoDeluxe file. The only drawback to layers is that they take up space and make a file bigger. See "Merging layers" on page 24 for a solution to this problem.

Island layer active

Text layer active

Naming layers

Layers that you create with the New button are named in the order in which they are created—Layer 1, Layer 2, and so on. If you're working with only one or two layers, keeping track of what's on each layer isn't a problem. But if you create several layers, and especially if you want to rearrange the layers, it's a good idea to give them descriptive names.

To name a layer as you create it, enter a name in the New Layer dialog box.

To rename a layer, double-click it in the Layer palette. The Layer Options dialog box appears.

Enter the new name.

Click OK to rename the layer.

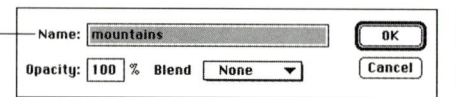

Rearranging layers

Often, the order in which you create layers is not the order in which you want to view them. For example, if you add a photo for a new background, you'll want to move that layer to the bottom of the Layers palette.

To move layers, drag the layer up or down in the Layers palette. A red arrow shows the new location of the layer. Release the mouse button to move the layer.

Viewing layers

When you're combining photos, you'll probably work with all the layers visible, so that you're seeing the entire collage. When you're using layers to try out different effects, such as alternate backgrounds, you might want to make individual layers visible or invisible so that you're seeing only some of the layers.

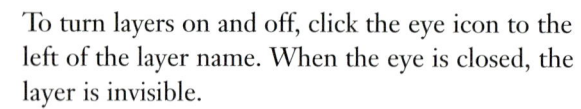

To turn layers on and off, click the eye icon to the left of the layer name. When the eye is closed, the layer is invisible.

Moving layers

To move the contents of a layer, make the layer you want to move the active layer, then click the Move tool and drag.

Displaying transparent areas of a layer

The parts of the layer that don't contain any pixels are transparent. Unless you change it, Adobe PhotoDeluxe shows these transparent areas as white. If you fill a selection with white, or if the photo contains white areas, it's easy to get confused about which parts of the layer are transparent (deleted) and which are not. For example, you might delete a background but not realize it's gone because it still appears as an opaque white area. To clearly differentiate transparent areas, you can change how Adobe PhotoDeluxe shows the transparency.

To change how transparent areas look on a layer, choose File>Preferences>Background.

Click a size to display transparent areas as a checkerboard.

Click to select colors for the checkerboard.

Choose a custom shade or color for the checkerboard.

Click OK to change the checkerboard.

No grid

Small grid size, gray and white

Medium grid size, contrasting colors

Underlying layers show through the transparent areas

> A quick way to select everything that's on a layer is to choose the Color Wand tool and click a transparent area. Click Add and continue clicking until you've selected all the transparent areas. Then click Invert to select all the areas that contain color.

Merging layers

While you're creating collages and editing an Adobe PhotoDeluxe file, layers provide the flexibility you need to try out different effects and rearrange elements. You can have up to six layers. If you find that you need more layers, you can **merge** one or more of the layers to combine them into one layer.

Because layers take up space and increase your file size, you might want to merge all the layers when you're finished working with the photo. **Flattening** the document (merging all the layers into one layer) creates a smaller file that takes up less space, prints faster, and takes less time to send via e-mail or for others to download.

Adobe PhotoDeluxe merges only *visible* layers (that is, layers that have their eye icon turned on). Once you've merged layers, they're gone—you can't separate the layers again.

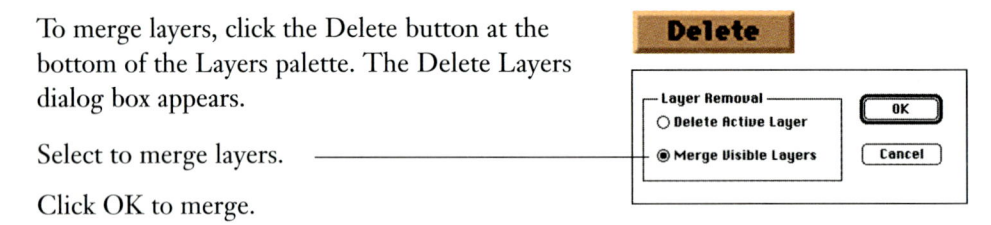

To merge layers, click the Delete button at the bottom of the Layers palette. The Delete Layers dialog box appears.

Select to merge layers.

Click OK to merge.

Deleting layers

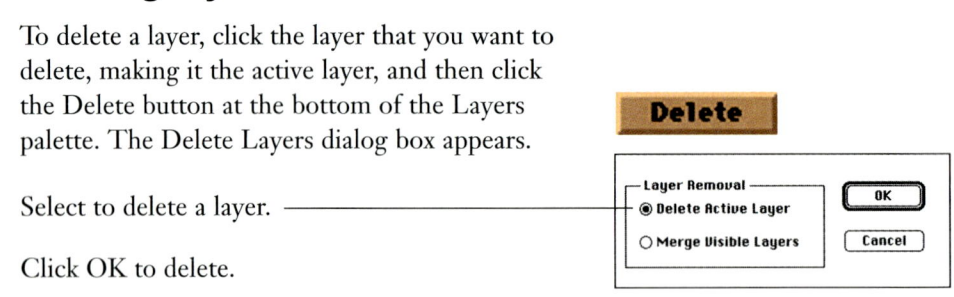

To delete a layer, click the layer that you want to delete, making it the active layer, and then click the Delete button at the bottom of the Layers palette. The Delete Layers dialog box appears.

Select to delete a layer.

Click OK to delete.

When you save an Adobe PhotoDeluxe file, all the layers are saved too, unless you specifically merge the layers before saving. If you think you might want to work on a photo again, don't merge the layers. YOU CAN'T UNMERGE LAYERS!

Changing the size and resolution of a photo

Once you scan a photo, the photo size (physical dimensions), the file resolution, and the file size are all linked together. For example, a 3 x 3 inch photo that's scanned at 72 ppi has a file size of 137 K. The same 3 x 3 inch photo scanned at 150 ppi has a file size of 594 K, and if it's scanned at 300 ppi, the file is 2.32 MB!

When you use the Trim and Resize buttons to change the size of a photo, Adobe PhotoDeluxe changes the photo size but keeps the original resolution. When you change the size of a photo with the Photo Size button, you have the option of changing or not changing its resolution. In most cases you won't want to change a photo's resolution.

> It's never a good idea to increase a photo's resolution in Adobe PhotoDeluxe because you inevitably get a blurry, lower-quality image.

When might you want to reduce the resolution? If you have a file that's been scanned at a high resolution (over 300 ppi), you might want to lower the resolution to match the resolution you need for output. Or you might want to have copies of a photo at different resolutions because you're going to print one copy, send another copy to a friend on e-mail, and put a third copy on your Web page. (See "Getting photos into Adobe PhotoDeluxe" on page 5 for information about setting scanning resolutions for different kinds of output.)

Sometimes you have files that are simply too big to work with on your computer. (Larger photos or files with higher resolutions are bigger, require more memory to work with, and require large amounts of disk space.) You can try reducing the size of the image first, but sometimes you need to reduce the resolution to get a file that you can use.

To find out the current size and resolution of an image, click the size box in the lower left corner of the Adobe PhotoDeluxe window. Hold down the mouse button to display the photo information.

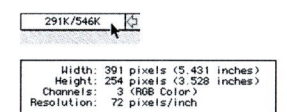

To change the image size, click Modify>Size>Photo Size. The Photo Size dialog box appears.

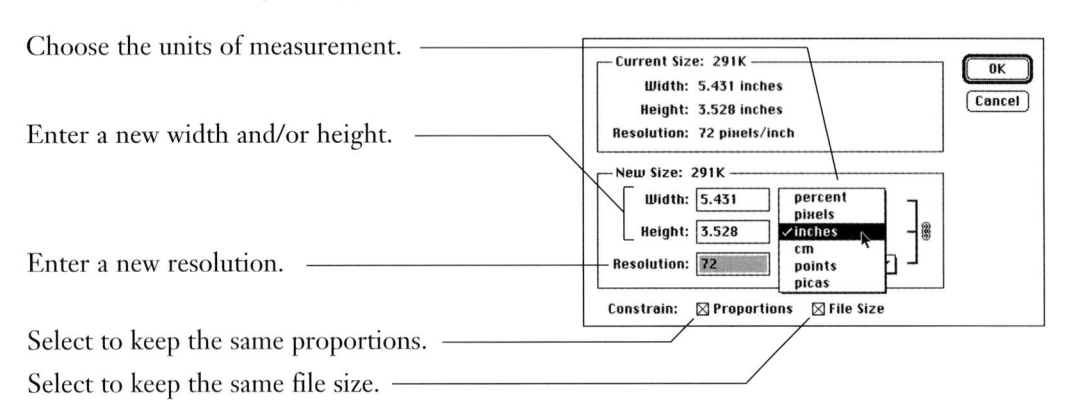

Choose the units of measurement.

Enter a new width and/or height.

Enter a new resolution.

Select to keep the same proportions.
Select to keep the same file size.

Click OK to change the size or resolution.

What you see is not necessarily what you get

No matter what the resolution of your photo, your monitor can display it at only one resolution. For Macintosh monitors, the resolution is set at 72 ppi. For Windows-compatible monitors, the resolution is usually 96 ppi (with some monitors you can vary the resolution).

Actual size
(scan resolution= 150ppi)

Display size
(screen resolution=72ppi)

Unless your screen resolution is exactly the same as the scan resolution, you don't see the photo at its actual size on the screen. For example, if your monitor displays 72 ppi and the scan resolution is 150 ppi, you see the image at approximately twice its actual width and height. (The monitor can only show 72 pixels in each inch, so it has to add enough inches to show all 150 pixels.) If the scan resolution is 150 ppi and your monitor resolution is 96 ppi, you see the image at closer to its actual size, although it will still be slightly larger on the screen.

Actual size
(scan resolution= 150ppi)

Display size
(screen resolution=96ppi)

Changing the magnification of a photo

Adobe PhotoDeluxe normally opens an image at 100% of its size. If the photo is too big to fit on your screen, the image may appear at 50% of its actual size. You can change the magnification of the photo by clicking the Zoom In and Zoom Out buttons above the Select palette on the left side of the Adobe PhotoDeluxe window. The zoom box shows the current magnification.

It's a good idea to zoom in when you're selecting irregular shapes or adding to or reducing selections. Zoom in to select with more precision.

Original size

Magnification = 200%

Zoom out to return to normal magnification, or to get an overview of a photo that doesn't all fit on the screen.

Original size

Magnification = 50%

Using menus

The Adobe PhotoDeluxe long menus give you an alternative way to use the Adobe PhotoDeluxe commands. If you prefer to work by choosing commands from menus instead of clicking buttons, you can turn on the complete set of menus by choosing File>Preferences>Long Menus.

When you use long menus, a few more options are available to you. For example, you can turn rulers on and off by choosing View>Show Rulers or View>Hide Rulers. You can also use Command-A to select all of an image and Command-D to deselect a selection. To turn off the menus, choose File>Preferences>Short Menus.

Saving and printing photos

When you're working in On Your Own, Adobe PhotoDeluxe provides four basic choices for saving your photos. To save a photo, click Save/Print, click the Save tab, and then click one of the following buttons.

	Saves a photo as an Adobe PhotoDeluxe file. Saving a photo as an Adobe PhotoDeluxe file keeps all the layers. When you're working on a photo project, you should save frequently—at least every 15 minutes!
	Stores a photo in the Hold Photo folder. Use this button when you want to combine photos or parts of photos. See "Holding photos" and "Retrieving photos" on page 19 for more information about using this feature.
	Saves a photo as an Acrobat PDF file. Save a file in this format to send an electronic copy to someone who doesn't have Adobe PhotoDeluxe, or to someone who has a different computer type than you (Macintosh, Windows, DOS, or UNIX). The PDF file can be read using the Adobe Acrobat Reader, which comes with Adobe PhotoDeluxe.
	Saves a photo and puts it in a screen-saver slide show. You can play this slide show on your computer screen whenever you're not using your computer. The slide show is an After Dark module. A copy of the After Dark screen-saver/slide show module is included with Adobe PhotoDeluxe.

You can print Adobe PhotoDeluxe photos on your own printer, or you can take your photos to a copy center to have them printed. Adobe PhotoDeluxe provides three printing choices. To print a photo, click Save/Print, click the Print tab, and then click one of the following buttons.

	Displays the Page Setup dialog box. These are the standard preview options that you get for all your applications. Select the options you want for printing the photo.
	Displays a preview of the photo, showing its placement on the page and any borders you may placed have around the photo.

Become an Instant Expert   29

Displays the Print dialog box. Enter the number of copies you want to print. You can print a selection or the entire photo. Only visible layers are printed.

You can also export Adobe PhotoDeluxe files in other file formats, such as GIF format for Web pages. For detailed information on saving and printing files, see Section 5, "Save, Print, and Store Photos."

Working efficiently

There are no complicated procedures or rules for working in Adobe PhotoDeluxe. The most important rule is to have fun! But there are a few things you can do that allow Adobe PhotoDeluxe to work at top speed and to help you get the most out of the program.

- Keep your files small. Use the lowest resolution that works for the output method you've chosen. See "Getting photos into Adobe PhotoDeluxe" on page 5 for more information.

- Merge layers to save disk space and reduce file size (but only when you're sure you won't need them again). See "Merging layers" on page 24 for details on how to merge.

- When you don't need them any more, turn off the Clue Cards. To turn off the display of all Clue Cards, choose File>Preferences>Turn Off All Clue Cards. You can always turn the cards back on if you find that you miss them.

- Turn off Macintosh Virtual Memory. See the Adobe PhotoDeluxe documentation for more information about assigning and using virtual memory.

- Assign more RAM to Adobe PhotoDeluxe. The program needs about 5 MB of memory to run. Assigning more memory lets it run faster and is particularly helpful when you're working with large files and performing some actions such as applying filters. See the Adobe PhotoDeluxe documentation for more information on assigning memory.

- Keep as much space free on your hard disk as possible. Adobe PhotoDeluxe uses your hard disk as a **scratch disk**. (The scratch disk is where Adobe PhotoDeluxe stores the photos and command instructions when you're making changes to a photo and there isn't enough room for this data in memory.) Adobe PhotoDeluxe needs at least as much free disk space as the RAM you have assigned to the program, and for some operations about three to five times the size of the file you're working on.

  Unless you change it, Adobe PhotoDeluxe uses the disk where the application is installed as the primary scratch disk. If you have another hard disk that is faster or has more room on it, you can assign it as your primary scratch disk. You can also assign a secondary scratch disk. To set the scratch disk options, choose File>Preferences>Scratch Disks. Don't use a removable disk, such as a Syquest cartridge, as your scratch disk. These disks are slower than a hard disk and they're also less reliable. See the Adobe PhotoDeluxe documentation for more information on setting scratch disk preferences.

- If you're going to be switching between applications, but you're not copying the Adobe PhotoDeluxe photo into other applications, choose File>Preferences>Export Clipboard and turn off the Export Clipboard option. Unless you change it, Adobe PhotoDeluxe saves the contents of the Clipboard whenever you leave the program. Because photos are so big, exporting the Clipboard can take a long time when you've cut or copied a photo.

SECTION 3

Everyday Uses

This section presents the techniques you need to correct those annoying everyday problems you have with photos—there's a scratch across your mother's face, you can't find a good picture of the entire family, Grandpa has a tree growing out of his head, your vacation photos turned out too dark—all the things that used to make you want to toss the photos in the trash. Well, Adobe PhotoDeluxe is here to help you solve these dilemmas, and others you haven't even thought of yet.

But this section offers more than just solutions—it also helps you to discover your hidden creative talents. You'll learn how to turn an ordinary picture into a personalized postcard, how to create text and graphic extravaganzas, and how to apply special effects that will leave your friends and family in awe.

So warm up that computer, make yourself comfortable, and begin your journey into the amazing world of Adobe PhotoDeluxe.

Removing flaws 32
Working on layers 36
Using the Hold Photo folder 41
Adding text to a photo 46
Using blend modes 51
Resizing selections 56
Revealing one photo through another 60
Creating silhouettes 64
Coloring drawings 68
Tinting a black-and-white photo 72
Filling text 77
Balancing color 82
Changing brightness and contrast 87
Retouching a face 92
Creating a business card 97
Filling selections 101
Creating a panorama 106
Using layers to try out effects 111
Color correcting a landscape 116
Using the scanner as a camera 121

Removing flaws

One of the easiest and most exciting uses of Adobe PhotoDeluxe is to restore old and damaged photographs. Besides fixing obvious flaws, such as the creases and tears in this photo, you can also balance faded colors and even reconstruct missing parts of a photo.

If the photo has several flaws, consider having it scanned at a copy center or service bureau. A professional scan can correct many problems during the scanning process and give you a better quality image to work with. If you do scan the photo yourself, try scanning several versions with different settings. For example, sometimes a scan with less contrast can help hide flaws; or a black-and-white scan might be more effective than one that's in color.

Restoring photos is a process of small, incremental changes. As you make corrections, try out each effect in stages so you can gauge the effect on the image. Moving in small steps also assures that you won't "over-correct" the photo and cause it to appear artificial or unnatural. In this example the crease is removed and a small missing piece of the face is repaired.

Removing flaws 33

1 Open the photo and select the area you want to fix

Click Get Photo>Open File and open the photo you want to fix.

When you're removing dust and scratches, you usually correct the entire photo (areas without flaws are not changed by the correction). If your photo has several damaged areas, some of which are much worse than others, you might want to select and correct individual areas. If you need to make a selection, click Modify and then select a tool from the Select palette.

2 Repair scratches

Remove Dust/Scratch searches the photo for areas where the color changes and then blurs the areas so they blend in with their surroundings.

To correct the scratch, you need to give Adobe PhotoDeluxe two pieces of information about the photo. First, you must decide how wide an area (radius) you want to blur. For example, a radius of 2 eliminates flaws up to 4 pixels thick. The smaller the radius, the less blurring in the photo.

Original photo

Too large of a radius blurs the details

Always use the smallest radius setting that eliminates the flaw. Larger values eliminate dust and scratches, but they can also blur important detail in the photo.

Second, you must also decide how different the color changes must be to be considered a flaw (threshold). If you leave the setting at 0, all the selected pixels are blurred. If you set it to 20, only pixels that vary by at least 20 color levels from the surrounding pixels are changed.

The threshold level can vary from 0 (no color difference between adjacent pixels) to 255 (the color must vary from pure white to pure black).

Adjust the radius first and then, if necessary, increase the threshold setting. Try different combinations of radius and threshold settings until you've reached a compromise between hiding the flaws and too much blurring.

Everyday Uses

Click Modify>Quality>Remove Dust/Scratch.

Drag to indicate the width of the blur.

Drag to indicate how different the colors should be to indicate a flaw.

Click OK to fix the scratch.

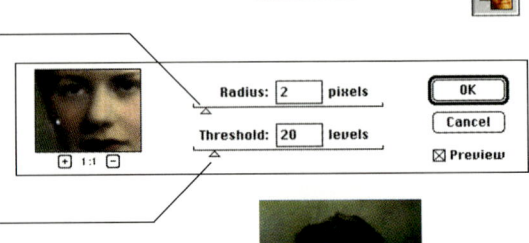

3 Repair irregular shapes

To fix a larger irregularly shaped area in a photo, the best technique is to select and copy a similarly shaped and colored area and then paste the selection over the flaw. In this example, the Trace tool was used to select an area to cover the tear.

Click Modify>Edit>Copy to copy the selection to the Clipboard

Click Edit>Paste to paste a copy over the selected area.

Drag the copy over the flaw.

4 Save the photo

Click Save/Print>Save>Save.

You're ready to print the photo, save it as an Acrobat file, save it in a slide show, or export it into another format to send it via e-mail or display it on the Internet or your personal Web page.

5 Variations

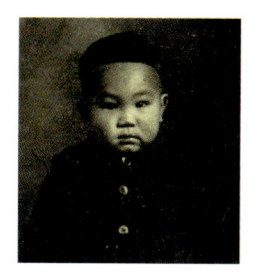

If the photo becomes too blurry, try reducing the selection area around the flaw.

When you need to repair a flaw, first try this selection, copy, and paste technique. If you can't fix the flaw, move on to the paint technique: select a fine brush, sample a color from the photo that's near the color you want, and paint over the flaw.

Working on layers

Combining effects is one area where Adobe PhotoDeluxe really lets your creativity shine. Not only can you combine photographs to make collages, you can also draw on photos to produce a mixed-media look. Using unexpected shapes, colors, and patterns, you can create unique and memorable images from ordinary photographs.

This technique uses Adobe PhotoDeluxe **layers.** Layers are like sheets of clear plastic stacked one on top of the other. When there's nothing on a layer, you can see right though it. When you add a selection or text, the space that is filled blocks the view of what's underneath. As long as things are on separate layers, you can move them around, change their color or opacity, or delete them entirely—all without affecting what's on the other layers. Layers make it easy to combine photos and effects and offer you an almost unlimited number of "undos." For a detailed discussion, see "Using layers" on page 20.

In this technique the appealing but rather bland photo of the dog was altered using the Adobe PhotoDeluxe selection tools. A border was added (resembling the mats often used in framed photos) to make the image stand out from its background. With a few simple changes, this image was changed into a perfect invitation for the pup's next whelpday party!

Working on layers 37

1 Open the photo you want to alter

Click Get Photo>Open File and open the photo you want to change.

When you open a photo in Adobe PhotoDeluxe, it has a single layer. This layer is often called the **background** because it's the layer that underlies all the layers you create. Adobe PhotoDeluxe names this layer Layer 0. If you open a sample photo, this layer may have a name, or it may be called Layer 1.

2 Create a new layer

By creating a separate drawing layer you can experiment with lots of different looks without changing the underlying layer. You can add up to six layers to a single photo.

To create a layer, click the New button at the bottom of the Layers palette.

Enter a name.

Click OK to create the layer.

(To rename an existing layer, double-click the layer in the Layers palette and then enter a new name in the dialog box.)

The new layer appears above the bottom layer in the Layers palette. The layer is green to show that it's the **active layer.** Whatever you do—paint, fill, delete, or move—it affects only the active layer; all the other layers stay just as they are.

3 Draw or paint on the layer

You can use any of the selection tools (except the Color Wand) to draw shapes on a layer. You can then fill the shapes with colors or patterns. In this photo the Polygon tool was used to draw the hat and bow tie.

You can also use the Brush, Line, Color Change, and Smudge tools to paint on the photo. Use small strokes so if you make a mistake you can undo just your last stroke.

Everyday Uses

To fill a drawn selection, click Modify>Effects>Selection Fill.

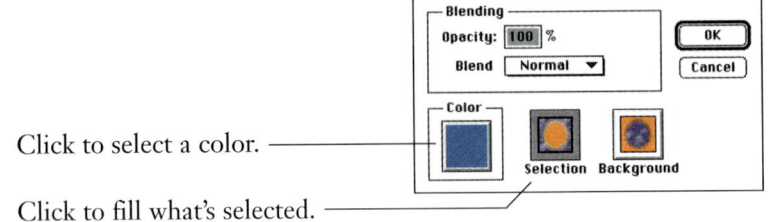

Click to select a color.

Click to fill what's selected.

Click OK to fill the selection.

To make corrections, drag to move the selection. Use the Eraser tool to erase areas you want to draw or paint again. Because the drawing is on its own layer, the underlying photo doesn't change when you move or erase.

4 Create the oval mat

Click in the Layers palette to make the layer with your photo the active layer. (In this example, it's the Dog layer.)

To draw an oval, choose the Oval tool from the pop-up menu in the Select palette and draw. If it's the wrong shape, click None in the Select palette and draw again. If it's the right shape but in the wrong place, hold down Command and Option as you drag the oval's selection border.

Working on layers 39

> You can't move a selection to a different place if the area is transparent, as it is on the painting layer in this example. If you tried to drag the oval, you would get a message that the selected area is empty. That's why you must press Command and Option to move the oval—you're moving the selection border, not the selected area.

Outlining the oval helps to separate it from the photo. Click Modify>Effects>Outline to outline the selection.

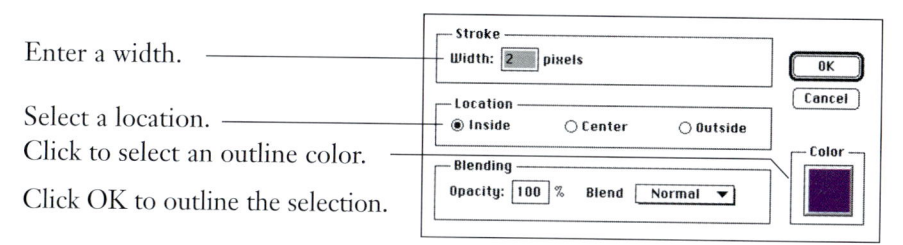

Enter a width.

Select a location.

Click to select an outline color.

Click OK to outline the selection.

As a final touch, you can delete the area outside of the oval to create a vignette effect. Click Modify>Edit>Delete Background.

> It's easy to get confused about when to use the Delete button and when to use the Delete Background button.
>
> When you click Delete Background, everything that is *not* selected gets deleted. When you click Delete, everything that *is* selected gets deleted.

5 Save the photo

Click Save/Print>Save>Save.

You're ready to print the photo, save it as an Acrobat file, save it in a slide show, or export it into another format to send it via e-mail or display it on the Internet or your personal Web page.

6 Variations

Adobe PhotoDeluxe allows only one selection at a time. This is why you must use the Add tool to add to an existing selection or the Reduce tool to delete from a selection. Every time you click a New tool and begin dragging, the old selection disappears.

If you want to fill a selection matching a color that already exists in the photo, click Modify>Effects>Selection Fill and then click the Color box. (Drag the dialog box by its title bar if you need to move it to see the image.) Click a color in the actual photo instead of choosing from the Color Swatches palette. When you close the Color Swatches palette, the color from the photo appears in the color box.

Using the Hold Photo folder

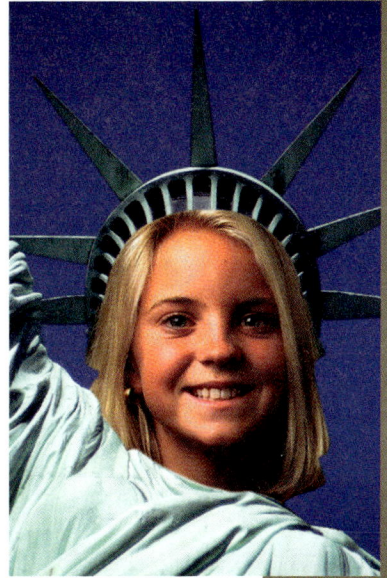

Adobe PhotoDeluxe can have only one photo open at a time. One way to combine photos is to copy and paste (copy one photo or a selection to the Clipboard, close the photo, open another photo, and paste.) The problem with this approach is that you can only have one item on the Clipboard. What if you want to try out several alternative photo combinations?

To have several photos available, you store the extra photos in the Hold Photo folder. You can retrieve these photos even if you already have an open photo. When you add a photo from the Hold Photo folder, Adobe PhotoDeluxe automatically puts it on a new layer. You can rearrange the photo combinations to your heart's content and still keep each layer intact. For more information, see "Using layers" on page 20.

This example uses parts of two photos. Combining sections of photos is a good way to make use of those "half-good" pictures that showcase some good features but also have parts you'd rather no one ever sees. Selecting parts of a photo also lets you make use of damaged photos that you might otherwise just throw away.

Everyday Uses

1 Open and edit the first photo

Sometimes when you're combining photos you can simply open one photo, put the other photo on top of it, and you're done. More often, however, you need to make adjustments to all the photos in a collage. In this example the face must be switched.

Click Get Photo>Open Photo to open the first photo.

In the statue photo the face needs to be deleted to make room for the girl's picture. This is an irregular shape, so the Trace tool was used to outline the statue's face.

The face was then deleted by clicking Modify>Edit>Delete.

Deleting the statue's face makes this area transparent (although it appears as opaque white). For information on changing how transparency appears in a layer, see "Displaying transparent areas of a layer" on page 23.

2 Save the first photo in the Hold Photo folder

Click Print/Save>Save>Hold Photo to store the photo. The photo is closed and you're ready to begin work on the next photo.

Once you save a photo in the Hold Photo folder, the Hold Photo bar appears on the left of the Adobe PhotoDeluxe window. Click this bar to retrieve your photo from the Hold Photo folder.

Using the Hold Photo folder   43

3 Open and edit the second photo

In this example, the second photo is not as tall as the first photo. Extra **canvas** (the space around a photo) must be added to the second photo so that there's enough room for the entire statue head in the final photo.

Click Get Photo>Open Photo to open the second photo.

To add canvas, click Modify>Size>Canvas Size.

Enter new dimensions. (In this example, the canvas height is increased by 1 inch and the width is increased by 2 inches.)

Click where you want the photo to appear in relation to the new canvas (in this example the photo will appear in the bottom center of the new canvas).

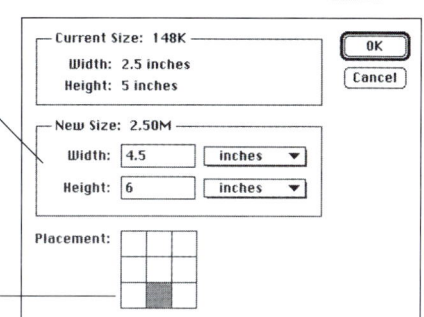

Click OK to add the canvas.

The canvas is added to the top of the photo. Depending on where you add the canvas, you might need to increase the window size. For example, if you add canvas above a photo, you might not see the entire photo in the window. To increase the window size, drag the box at the lower right corner of the Adobe PhotoDeluxe window.

4 Get the photo from the Hold Photo folder

When you're ready to combine the photos, click the Hold Photo button above the Layers palette.

The contents of the Hold Photo folder appear in a window under your open photo. To move the Hold Photo window to a more convenient location, drag its title bar. To resize the Hold Photo window, drag the box at the lower right corner.

To combine the photos, drag the photo over the open window. (You can also select the photo and then click the Paste Layer button or double-click the photo.)
As you release the mouse button, the Make Layer dialog box appears. Adobe PhotoDeluxe automatically makes a new layer when you add photos from the Hold Photo folder.

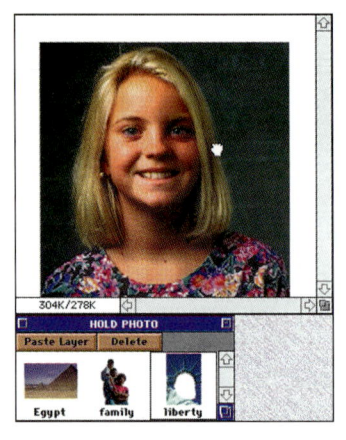

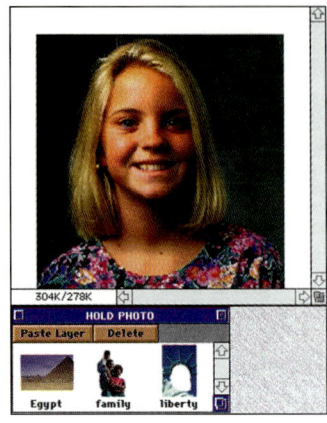

Name the layer and then click OK.

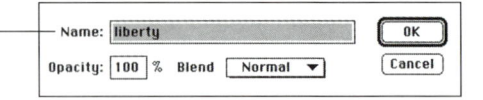

The photo from the Hold Photo folder appears on top of the original photo in the center of the window. The layer for the added photo appears at the top of the Layers palette; it is now the active layer. Your image has two photos, each on a separate layer.

5 Edit the combined photo

Once you have the photos in the same window, you'll probably have to do some editing. In this example the girl's face needs to be moved into position. Then the photo needs to be trimmed to cut out extra or overlapping areas.

Using the Hold Photo folder   45

Click the Move tool and drag the layer you need to position. Only the active layer moves.

To trim the photos, click Modify>Size>Trim. Drag a selection around the part of the photo you want to keep. Click inside the selection with the OK cursor to trim, or outside the selection with the cancel cursor to try again.

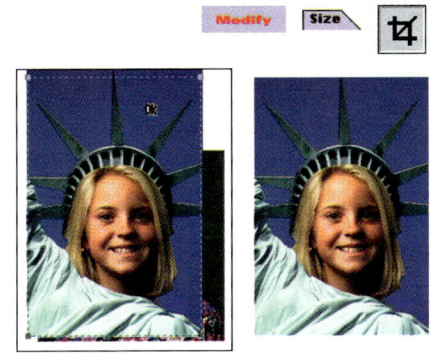

6 Save the photo

Click Save/Print>Save>Save.

You're ready to print the photo, save it as an Acrobat file, save it in a slide show, or export it into another format to send it via e-mail or display it on the Internet or your personal Web page.

7 Variations

Be the first golfer on the moon    Let the lion lie down with the cat    Call on the wisdom of the ancients

> To make tiny adjustments as you move a layer, press an arrow key on the keyboard. This moves the layer 1 pixel at a time. To make slightly larger jumps, hold down Shift and press an arrow key. This moves the layer 10 pixels at a time.

Adding text to a photo

Adding text to a photo can be informative (such as reminding you of the name of a castle you visited in Ireland, or identifying which niece this is and what grade she's in), essential (such as displaying your company or product name), or decorative (such as jazzing up an otherwise ordinary picture with an interesting message or literary quotation).

When you're entering text on a photo, there are a few things that you can do to make the text more effective.

- Limit the text to as few words as possible. Too much text can overwhelm the photo.
- Use only one or two typefaces or sizes. Too many effects make the text confusing.
- Be sure the text is large enough to read easily.
- Place the text on a neutral or solid-colored background.

With Adobe PhotoDeluxe you cam create horizontal and vertical text. You can fill the text with a solid color, a gradient, or even part of another photo. You can mix and match the type, size, and colors. While restraint is the rule of thumb, rules were made to be broken—so go ahead and create the most garish and untasteful combinations of text you can think of!

This example combines two photos and adds both vertical and horizontal text to create a personalized postcard. You can use this technique to add text to any photo, including captions, invitations, posters, calendars, or greeting cards.

Adding text to a photo 47

1 Create the background for the text

Open the photo you're going to use behind the text. If you're using multiple photos, make any necessary selections or corrections and copy one photo to the Clipboard or store the extra photos in the Hold Photo folder.

In this example two photos were combined to make the background. The family was selected by first using the Color Wand to select the sky. The selection was then inverted to select the family.

The background was deleted using the Feather button. When you feather as you fill or delete a selection, you create soft edges, so that the selection blends in more gradually when you paste it into a new location.

To delete using a feathered edge, click Modify>Effects> Feather.

Enter a value to indicate how wide the soft edge should be.

Click to delete what is not selected.

Click OK to delete the background.

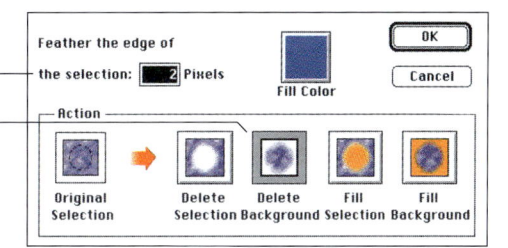

The feathered selection was copied to the Clipboard, the landscape photo was opened, and the selection was pasted into the second photo. After positioning the pasted family, the selection was deselected using the None button.

2 Create the horizontal text

With the Text button you can put text anywhere in a photo. When you enter text, you select its style, alignment, font, size, color, and placement. Adobe PhotoDeluxe puts the text on a separate layer so you can adjust it before making a permanent part of the photo. Adobe PhotoDeluxe comes with twelve Adobe fonts, but you can use any font that's installed on your computer.

To enter the text, click Modify>Tools>Text.

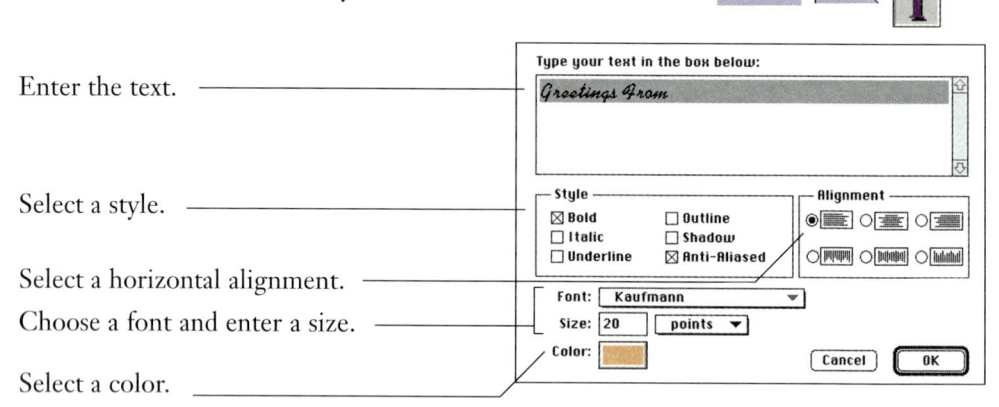

Enter the text.

Select a style.

Select a horizontal alignment.

Choose a font and enter a size.

Select a color.

Click OK to add the text.

The text appears as a selection in the photo and a Text layer appears in the Layers palette. The Text layer is the active layer.

Because the text is on a separate layer, you can move it to to any location without disturbing the photo underneath. Make sure the Text layer is active and use the Move tool to drag the text into position.

Adding text to a photo 49

3 Create the vertical text

You can enter vertical text as well as horizontal text. This means you can run text down the side of a photo or even around the edges. When you add more text to a photo, it's added to the existing Text layer.

To enter the second set of text, click Modify>Tools>Text.

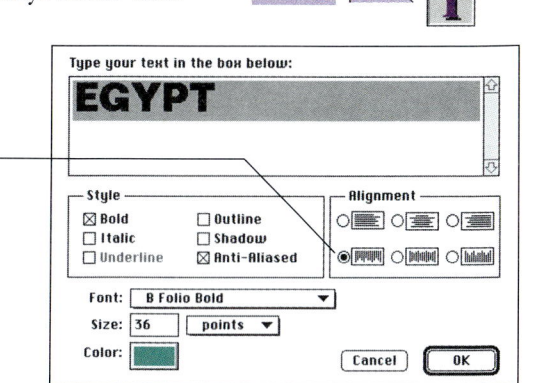

Enter the text.

Select a style.

Select a vertical alignment.

Choose a font and enter a size.

Select a color.

Click OK to add the text.

4 Resize the text

Text is just like any other Adobe PhotoDeluxe selection. Until you deselect it by clicking None in the Select palette, you can fill it with another color, give it an outline, or do any of the things you normally do to selections. You might find that once you have your text in place you want to resize it. For example, the vertical text in this photo is a bit overwhelmed by the pyramid, so it was resized to make it fatter.

Click Modify>Size>Free Resize. (Free Resize lets you adjust the height and width independently.)

Drag a handle to change the height or width.

Click inside the selection with the OK cursor to resize, or click outside the selection with the cancel cursor to try again.

Click None in the Select palette to see the text without the selection border. You can no longer resize the text or change its color, but you can still move the Text layer.

5 Save the photo

Click Save/Print>Save>Save.

You're ready to print the photo, save it as an Acrobat file, save it in a slide show, or export it into another format to send it via e-mail or display it on the Internet or your personal Web page.

6 Variations

Add canvas and label school photos

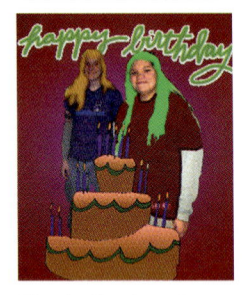

Use the Brush tool to add handwritten text

Personalize the message to Mom and Dad

When you paste one selection into another there is often a very sharp, noticeable edge between the two areas. That's why you might want to feather when you fill or delete a selection. Unless you enter a very large value in the Feather dialog box, it's often hard to see any feathering effect. Basically, that's the idea—you don't want to see the seams between selections. Of course, adding a lot of feathering is a cool way to make a blurry edge around a selection.

her value = 0    Feather value = 3    Feather value = 15

Using blend modes

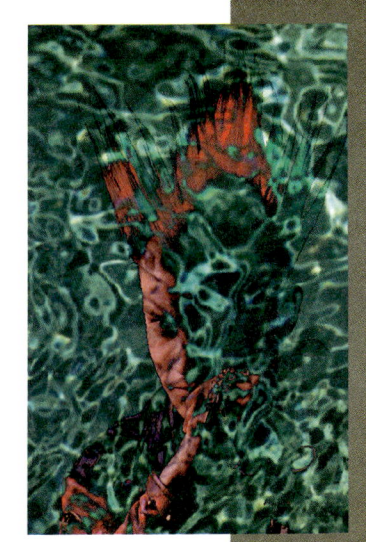

This technique introduces the Adobe PhotoDeluxe blends. Blends determine how the pixels in the photo combine with one another. On a single layer, you can set a blend when you fill a selection. You can also set blends for entire layers.

If you don't use a blend when you fill a selection, the fill color pixels replace the existing pixels. You see the new color in whatever opacity you're using. If you don't set a layer blend, each pixel in the topmost layer replaces all the underlying pixels and shows only the top layer's colors. It's when you *do* set blends that you see some very interesting color combinations.

Using blends doesn't require any technical expertise or artistic talent. You just try it out and see if you like the results. Here are some general descriptions of the blend settings.

- Normal — the fill or layer color covers the underlying color.
- Darken — intensifies the color.
- Lighten — fades the color.
- Overlay — combines the two colors without losing detail (mostly affects middle tones).
- Difference — combines the two colors, resulting in a new color.
- Color — tints the photo with the new color.

Everyday Uses

1 **Open the photo and fill a selection**

Click Get Photo>Open Photo to open the photo.

Click Modify and then choose a selection tool from the pop-up menu on the Select palette. In this example the Rectangle tool was used.

To set blend modes for individual selections, click Modify>Effects>Selections Fill.

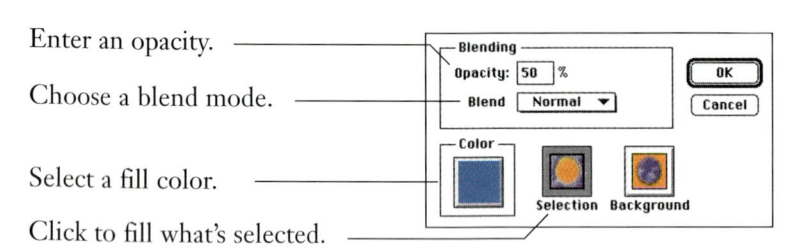

Enter an opacity.

Choose a blend mode.

Select a fill color.

Click to fill what's selected.

Click OK to fill.

By overlapping selections, varying the opacity, and applying multiple fills to the same areas you can produce an unlimited variety of interesting effects.

50% opacity, Normal mode

80% opacity, Darken mode

30% opacity, Lighten mode

v mode

80% opacity, Difference mode

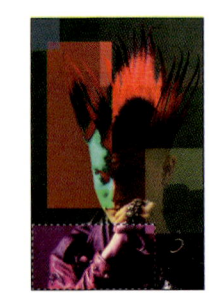

60% opacity, Color mode

Using blend modes 53

2 Create layers with different blend modes

When you set a blend mode for a layer, all the selections on that layer have the same blend mode. You must have at least two layers to see the effect of a layer blend setting.

To set or change a layer blend, choose a blend when you create the layer using the New button, or double-click the layer name in the Layers palette to display the Layer Options dialog box.

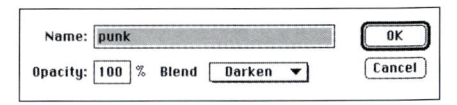

In this example the old background was deleted. A water texture was copied and pasted to a new layer to serve as the new background. The water was placed on a layer with no blend mode and moved to the bottom of the Layers palette. Then the top layer (the punk) was blended using different modes. Finally, the punk was pasted onto several layers, which were created with different blends. The layers were moved individually to produce the offset effect.

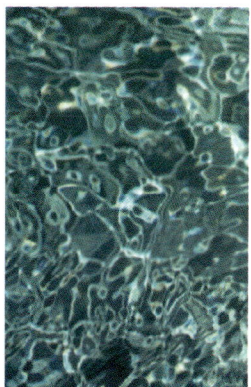

54 Everyday Uses

Normal   Darken   Lighten   Overlay

Difference   Color   Difference over colored selection   Color, Lighten, Darken on separate layers

3 Save the photo

Click Save/Print>Save>Save.

You're ready to print the photo, save it as an Acrobat file, save it in a slide show, or export it into another format to send it via e-mail or display it on the Internet or your personal Web page.

Using blend modes

4 Variations

Most of the blend modes correspond to a technique that can be performed in the real world. Darken, for example, is like printing a photo on a piece of translucent film and laying it over a photographic print (or for individual selections like drawing on a photo with magic markers). Wherever the colors mix, they are darkened. Try using the Darken blend to increase the density of overexposed photos or to apply shadows without eliminating the color of the shaded areas in the underlying layers.

Lighten produces the opposite effect and is like projecting two slides onto the same screen. Wherever the colors mix, they are lightened. Lighten is a good blend for applying highlights to an photo.

The Difference and Overlay blends can only occur in the world of computers. Applying Difference creates a photo negative that is the inversion of the blended images according to their color. Overlay darkens the dark colors and lighten the light ones, increasing the contrast and color saturation. Go figure!

When you use the Color mode, the hue and saturation of the colors are changed but the lightness (or luminosity) is not affected. This produces a look similar to colorizing old black-and-white movies.

Resizing selections

Sometimes it's fun to apply effects to an entire photo and see how dramatically it can change the image. But changing only part of a photo really opens up creative possibilities. Think of this technique as a visual exaggeration—how big was the fish you caught, or the horse you rode, or the bear you stared down? Do you dream of a bigger dog, a larger house, giant caterpillars, or smaller feet? With Adobe PhotoDeluxe, it's no problem.

There are several ways to resize a selection. If you want to remain in the realm of the realistic, you can use the Resize button to enlarge or shrink the object but keep its original proportions. If you want to hang out in the land of the fantastic, try resizing using the Distort and Perspective buttons.

In this technique the fish was resized and then sharpened slightly. When you make something bigger in a photo, Adobe PhotoDeluxe has to fill in the space with additional pixels. Sometimes these added pixels can make the resized selection look blurry. Sharpening a photo restores it almost to its original sharpness.

Resizing selections 57

1 **Open the photo and select the areas you want to resize**

Click Get Photo>Open Photo to open the photo.

Click Modify and then choose a selection tool from the pop-up menu on the Select palette. In this example the Color Wand tool and Trace tool were used to select the fish.

To Adobe PhotoDeluxe, the grays and pastels in this photo are similar colors. To avoid selecting too much with the Color Wand, the tolerance was lowered to about 15 before making the selection. The Trace tool was then used to add and reduce areas until there was a clean outline of the fish.

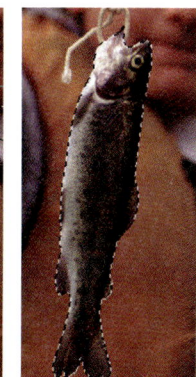

2 **Resize the selection**

When you resize, you can use either the Free Resize button or the Resize button. Use Free Resize to change the width and height independently. Use Resize to keep the same proportions as you scale the selection.

Click Modify>Size>Free Resize.

In this example Free Resize was used so that the fish could be made longer but not wider.

The handles were dragged independently to resize the selection. To resize, click inside the box with the OK cursor. To cancel the resizing and try again, click outside the box with the cancel cursor.

Everyday Uses

3 Sharpen the resized selection

Click Modify>Quality>Sharpen.

To restore the object's sharpness, sharpen the selection before you deselect it. In this image, sharpening the fish makes it stand out even more because the sense of depth is increased by the out-of-focus background.

Each time you click the Sharpen button, the selection is sharpened a little more.

4 Save the photo

Click Save/Print>Save>Save.

You're ready to print the photo, save it as an Acrobat file, save it in a slide show, or export it into another format to send it via e-mail or display it on the Internet or your personal Web page.

5 Variations

Carve the biggest turkey known to man

Over-sharpen to produce a toxic fish

Create a *real* watch dog

Resizing selections 59

In the technique in this example the photographer used a shallow "depth of field" setting to blur the boy in the background. This tends to emphasize foreground objects and make them look bigger as well as sharper. To use digital depth of field in your photos, select the background and then click Modify>Effects>Special Effects>Blur>Soften.

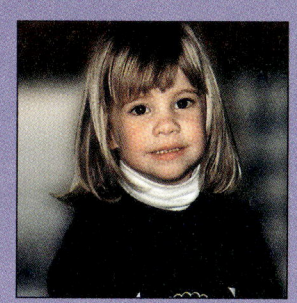

If you have some white areas around the object after it's resized and sharpened, deselect it and click Modify>Tools>Brush. Select a small, soft-edged brush from the Brushes palette. Click the color box and then click in the photo to select a paint color to fill in the white areas. Zoom in and use short strokes to touch up the photo. Click Undo if you accidentally paint over the object itself.

Each time you click the Sharpen button the sharpness is increased. To be sure you've got the right degree of sharpness, over-sharpen a bit (the selection will begin to look artificial), then click Undo to move back one level of sharpness.

Revealing one photo through another

It's not always necessary to make complex selections, store photos in the Hold Photo folder, and create layers to combine two photos. Adobe PhotoDeluxe has a feature called Paste Into that lets you show part of one image through another without adding more layers. This can produce the eerie translucent effect shown in the Halloween Cat.

Because creating layers requires additional steps and takes up disk space, copying and pasting is a quick and efficient way to combine images (as long as you only need two photos available at one time). Copying to the Clipboard can be a problem when the photo file is very large. In that case, make a selection of the part of the image that you need and copy only that section to the Clipboard.

Using an entire photo is also helpful when it would be hard to make a selection of a shape. In this example it would be difficult to select the pumpkin because it's not a regular shape and would be hard to trace; nor does it have sharp color contrast, so the Color Wand wouldn't work either. To create this image, it's much easier to select the black cat and then paste the entire pumpkin image into the cat selection. Moving the pumpkin photo lets you reveal just the part of the pumpkin you want to see.

Revealing one photo through another

1 Open the photo and select what you want to show through

Click Get Photo>Open Photo to open the first file.

You need to copy the photo that you want to reveal onto the Clipboard so that it's available when you open the second photo. (Adobe PhotoDeluxe can only have one photo open at a time.)

2 Copy the selection and close the photo

Click Modify>Edit>Copy to copy the photo.

Because the entire image is selected, the selection border appears around the edges of the photo.

After copying, close the photo and don't save the changes.

3 Open the second photo and select the see-through area

Click Get Photo>Open Photo to open the photo that will provide the background.

In order for one photo to show through another, you need to select the area that will contain the second image. Adobe PhotoDeluxe uses this selection border as a frame and shows only the part of the pasted photo that falls within the selection border.

In this example the cat provides the boundaries for the pasted pumpkin. To prepare this photo for the pumpkin, first the the Color Wand was used to select the background.

Before switching the selection to the cat, a little mystery was added to the photo by applying a special effect—some noise was added to make the background look grainy. (Noise is random pixels added to a selected area.)

Everyday Uses

Click Modify>Effects>Special Effects>Blur>
Noise. The Noise dialog box appears.

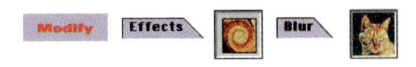

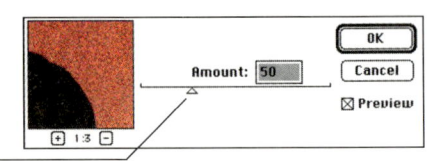

Drag the slider to change the amount.

Click OK to add the effect.

Click the Done tab to leave the Special Effects area return to the other Modify buttons.

With the background blurred, the Invert button was clicked to switch the selection to the cat.

4 Paste and position the copied selection

With the see-through area selected, you're ready to paste in the selection that you want to show through the background selection.

Click Modify>Edit>Paste Into.

When you use Paste Into, the window shows the border of the selection you're pasting. In this case the cat photo is bigger than the pumpkin photo. The pumpkin must be made larger to fill the cat.

Revealing one photo through another

To resize a pasted selection, click Modify>Size>Free Resize.

To resize, click inside the box with the OK cursor. To cancel the resizing and try again, click outside the box with the cancel cursor.

5 Save the photo

Click Save/Print>Save>Save.

You're ready to print the photo, save it as an Acrobat file, save it in a slide show, or export it into another format to send it via e-mail or display it on the Internet or your personal Web page.

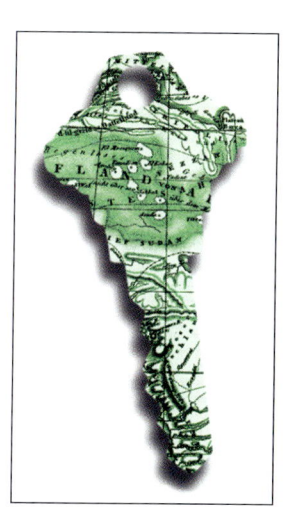

6 Variations

The Paste Into command is handy for replacing a selection you accidentally cut (when you can't use Undo) or for placing a copied selection exactly on top of itself.

Creating silhouettes

Vacations hold such promise! But sometimes when those eagerly awaited photos come back, you find that what you experienced as fantastic seems a little dull. That amazing ocean view looks foggy and overcast. Your great shot of the Eiffel Tower shows only green bushes—quite similar to those in your own back yard.

One simple way to add drama to a photo is to create a silhouette. Silhouettes are particularly effective in emphasizing a scene or activity and are a quick way to eliminate unwanted detail from a photo. You don't have to limit silhouettes to people and you don't have to limit the color to black—you can silhouette any solid shape in any dark color to produce interesting and unique effects.

If you're going to move the silhouette to another photo, look at the placement of the people or object in the original photo and compare it to the new photo. Is the photo vertical or horizontal? Do you want the shape to dominate or be a minor part of the image? Does the new photo have a big enough bright area to provide contrast for the silhouette? Visualizing the effect before you start combining images saves time when you're actually creating your masterpiece.

Creating silhouettes 65

1 Open the photo and select the shape

Click Get Photo>Open Photo to open the photo that contains the shape you're going to silhouette.

Probably the hardest part of creating a silhouette is selecting the shape. The good news, however, is that you don't have to worry about being precise in the selection; it's the overall shape that is important. In most cases, the easiest way to select the shape is to select what you don't want and then invert the selection.

In this example the ocean background was selected using the Color Wand and Trace tools. The Invert button in the Select palette was used to reverse the selection so that the couple was selected.

Sometimes when you're making a complex selection, it's difficult to tell what is selected. Just remember that everything between the dotted lines is selected. For example, in the photo on the left the dotted lines are around the outside of the photo and around the couple. Everything between the outside edge and the couple is selected. In the photo on the right, the dotted lines are around the couple and only they are selected.

2 Fill the shape with black and copy the selection to the Clipboard

With the outline selected, all you need to do to create the silhouette is to fill the shape with a dark color.

Click Modify>Effects>Selection Fill.

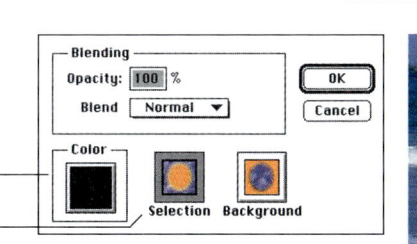

Select the fill color.

Click to fill what's selected.

Click OK to create the silhouette.

If you're going to paste the silhouette into another photo, click Modify>Edit>Copy to copy the silhouette to the Clipboard and then close the photo.

3 Open the new background photo and paste the selection

Click Get Photo>Open Photo to open the photo that will provide the background.

Click Modify>Edit>Paste to paste the selection into the photo.

When there is no selection in a photo, Adobe PhotoDeluxe pastes a selection into the center of the photo. (If there is a selection, the pasted selection is placed over the existing selection.)

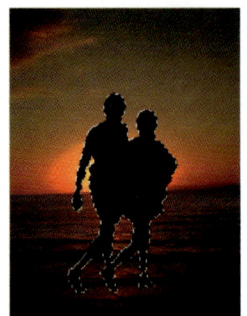

Drag the selection into place.

Because the two photos are about the same size, it was easy to place the silhouette in the new photo. You can resize a silhouette selection without worrying about distortion because you don't see any detail anyway. It's best to use the Resize button to resize so that the selection keeps its original proportions.

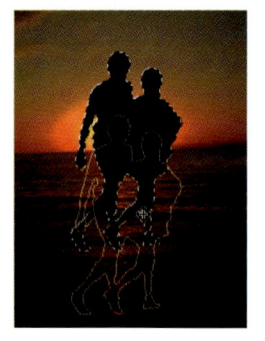

4 Save the photo

Click Save/Print>Save>Save.

You're ready to print the photo, save it as an Acrobat file, save it in a slide show, or export it into another format to send it via e-mail or display it on the Internet or your personal Web page.

Creating silhouettes

5 **Variations**

When you're trying to decide if you should copy a photo to the Clipboard and then paste it into another image or store the photo in the Hold Photo folder, consider what you want to do once you put the photo into the new image. If you want to make further adjustments, then you need to have the photo on a separate layer and should store it in the Hold Photo folder. If you're simply going to place the selection into another image, it's quicker and easier to copy and paste.

Coloring drawings

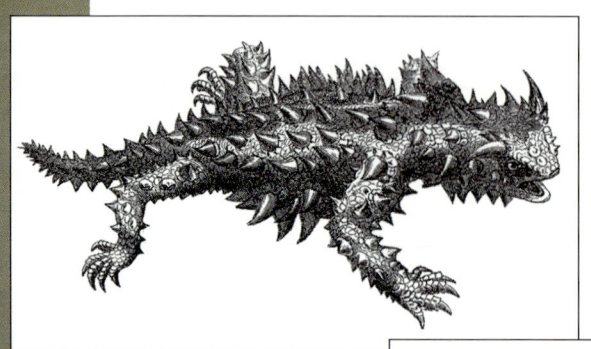

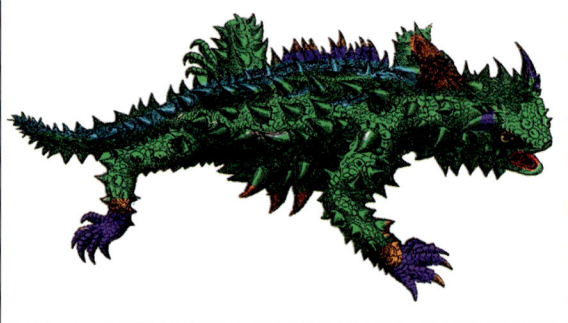

One of the easiest ways to add a unique touch to your cards, invitations, and flyers is to include drawings in addition to or instead of photos. You can draw the art yourself and scan it in, or you can create it in an art program and then open it in Adobe PhotoDeluxe.

If you can't draw a stick figure, don't despair! Many bookstores carry books of copyright-free black-and-white and grayscale drawings, such as those in the Dover series. You can also use electronic **clip art** collections of images available on floppy disk or CD-ROM that cover just about every imaginable subject. Ask your computer dealer for some clip art catalogs.

The lizard used in this technique was scanned in from a book of drawings. When you open a black-and-white or grayscale scan in Adobe PhotoDeluxe, the program automatically converts it into the color Adobe PhotoDeluxe format. Then you can add color—this lizard was painted using the Brush tool.

Selecting the area that you want to paint gives you the freedom to paint with abandon; the selection border keeps you from painting "outside of the lines." By making new selections, you can easily control where and how the paint is applied.

Coloring drawings 69

1 **Open the photo and select the object you want to color**

Click Get Photo>Open Photo to open the file.

If your line art comes from a book (of copyright-free images, or course!), part of other art may be included in the photo. In that case, use the Eraser tool to clean up the scan. (You can also erase by selecting the area with a selection tool and pressing the Delete key on your keyboard.)

Click Modify, choose a selection tool from the pop-up menu on the Select palette, and then select the object. A selection extends through all the layers. You can switch from layer to layer and still have the same selection border.

In this example the drawing is against a solid white background, so the Color Wand tool was used to select the background. The selection was then inverted to select the drawing.

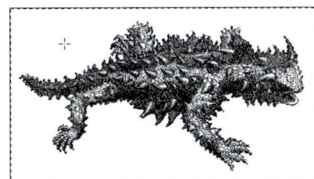

2 **Create a painting layer and choose a blend**

Creating a separate painting layer lets you try out different painting approaches without affecting the drawing on the bottom layer. One of the effects you can vary is the blending of the layers.

In this example the layer was created using the Overlay blend. Overlay mixes the color in the two layers. The dark and light areas don't change as much as the middle tones. Painting on an Overlay layer lets the texture of the drawing show though the paint. See "Using blend modes" on page 51 for a discussion of all the different blends.

Click the New button in the Layers palette to create the layer.

Enter a name.

Choose Overlay.

Click OK to create the layer.

The new layer appears in the Layers palette. You don't see any change on your screen because the new layer is empty (completely transparent).

3 Paint on the layer

Whenever you're painting, it's a good idea to use small strokes so that you can easily undo the last stroke if you don't like the effect. There's nothing more frustrating than working for a long time on a painting and then messing up right at the end. This is also a good reason to save frequently when you're painting.

Click Modify>Tools>Brush.

To paint the selection, select a brush size and a color from the Color Swatches palette and start painting.

Select different areas and try out different brush sizes, different colors, and other buttons such as the Smudge and Color Change buttons.

4 Try out other blends

You can quickly see how the painting looks using other blend mode settings. Changing the blend setting of the layer can give you some very surprising results!

Double-click the painting layer name in the Layers palette and then choose a new blend mode from the pop-up menu in the dialog box.

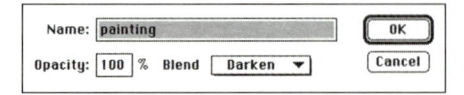

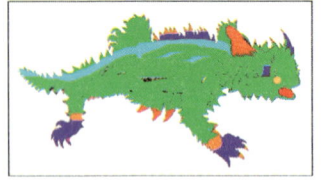

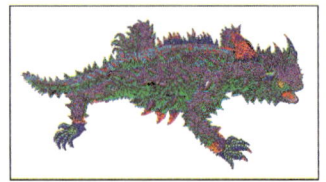

Normal blend   Darken blend   Difference blend

Coloring drawings 71

5 Save the photo

Click Save/Print>Save>Save.

You're ready to print the photo, save it as an Acrobat file, save it in a slide show, or export it into another format to send it via e-mail or display it on the Internet or your personal Web page.

6 Variations

Add the drawing to another photo

Create unknown species

Create a coloring book effect

To vary the opacity while you're painting, use the Selection Fill tool. If you want all the paint to have the same opacity (other than 100%), you can change the opacity of the layer.

You can look at the layers separately by turning them on or off. To see that your painting has not changed the original drawing, click the eye icon on the Painting layer.

Just for fun, click again to turn the Painting layer on and click the eye icon on the bottom layer to turn off the original drawing, so that you see just your painting strokes.

Sometimes the painting layer looks so good you might want to delete the original drawing layer and use just the painting layer as an illustration on a card or calendar! However, if you want to return to your painted art, turn on both layers. Merge the layers before saving.

Tinting a black-and-white photo

If you're a member of the baby-boom generation, you probably have a large collection of black-and-white photos. These photos are undeniably charming, but many can be made more compelling by the addition of color.

There are several ways to add color to a black-and-white photo. You can fill selections with color, use brushes to paint in color, create a sketch and color it, or add a tint. Tinting is by far the quickest method. Because the entire photo is tinted, you don't have to make any selections and you use only one color. Tinting produces an effect similar to the duotones you see in some newsletters and magazines.

The color of the tint radically changes the look of the photo. A brown color produces a sepia tone. (**Sepia** is a term that covers a lot of ground, from yellow-brown to blue-purple.) You can tint black-and-white photos to match existing sepia images, or you can retint photos to get consistent color for a group of photos you want to display together. Tinting with other colors, such as blue or green, also produces interesting effects.

The secret of realistic tinting is to color the photo with an opacity of less than 100% to keep all the detail of the original photo. In this example, the photo is tinted with brown. To reinforce the old-fashioned look, the tinted photo is cropped and enclosed in a vignette.

Tinting a black-and-white photo 73

1 Open the photo and sharpen it

Click Get Photo>Open File and open the photo you want to tint.

Click Modify>Quality>Sharpen to sharpen the photo.

When you're working with old photographs, it's generally a good idea to sharpen them. Sharpening can make up for the deficiencies of old cameras—or harried parents who tried to get the photo before you moved!

2 Create a new layer

The new layer will contain the tint for the photo. By putting the color on a layer, you can try out different colors without affecting the original photo. When you're applying a tint, use an opacity of less than 100%, so that the photo can show through the tint layer. Setting the layer blend to Lighten gives a faded look when you add the tint. (See "Using blend modes" on page 51 for more information about layer blends.)

To create the layer, click the New button in the Layers palette.

Name the layer.
Enter a percentage for the opacity.
Choose Lighten.
Click OK to create the layer.

3 Fill the layer

There are many ways you can fill this layer with color. Here's one you might not have tried yet. When you click the Color Change button and then click in the photo, Adobe PhotoDeluxe fills in all the space until it runs into another color. In this case there isn't any other color on the layer, so the whole layer is filled.

Click Modify>Tools>Color Change. Click the color box and then select a color for the tint from the Color Swatches palette. Click in the photo to add the color.

4 Save the photo

Once you have the color you want, click the Delete button at the bottom of the Layers palette and merge the layers. Click Save/Print>Save>Save to save the photo.

5 Add a vignette

For an old-fashioned look, you can create a vignette for your photo. Click Modify and select the Oval tool to draw the vignette shape. If you don't get the shape you want, click None to deselect and try again.

> You can also deselect by clicking anywhere in the photo outside of the selection border.

If you have the right shape, but it's in the wrong location, press Option and Command and drag the selection border to the position you want.

To finish the vignette, you need to get rid of the area outside the oval. To create a soft edge, so that the oval seems to bleed into the background, you can apply a feathered edge to the selection as you delete the background.

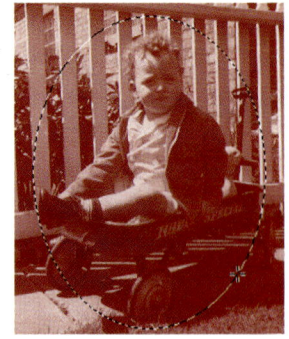

Tinting a black-and-white photo 75

You must merge the layers before you can create the vignette. If you don't, when you delete the area outside the oval you see the original black-and-white photo instead of a white background.

To create the feathered edge, click Modify>Effects>Feather.

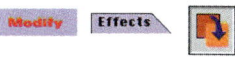

Enter a number to indicate how wide you want the soft edge to be.

Don't select a color (it will be white automatically).

Click to delete the area outside of the oval.

Click OK to create the vignette.

Click None in the Select palette to see the finished vignette. Don't forget to save the photo after you've finished all your changes.

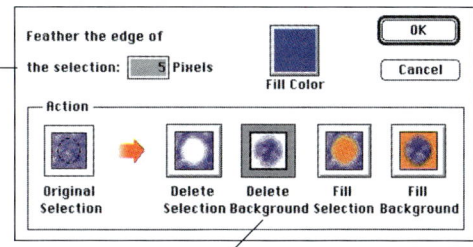

6 Variations

To tint a color photo, make a copy of the photo, then click Modify>Effects>Color to BW to create a black-and-white version of the color photo.

You can think of the Change Color button as the opposite of the Color Wand. The Color Wand tool selects areas of similar color; the Color Change buttons fills areas of similar color. The Color Change button uses the same tolerance setting as the Color Wand.

You could try out tints on the original photo, but you would need to undo the effect each time you wanted to try out a new color. By creating layers, you can put a different color on each layer and then turn the layers on and off to check out the different effects. To turn layers on and off, click the eye icon to the left of the layer name in the Layers palette. If you want the final effect to include colors from two layers, be sure that only those layers are visible when you merge the layers. Adobe PhotoDeluxe merges only visible layers. The others layers remain and must be deleted individually to reduce the file size.

Click the eye icon to view one or all of the layers

Filling text

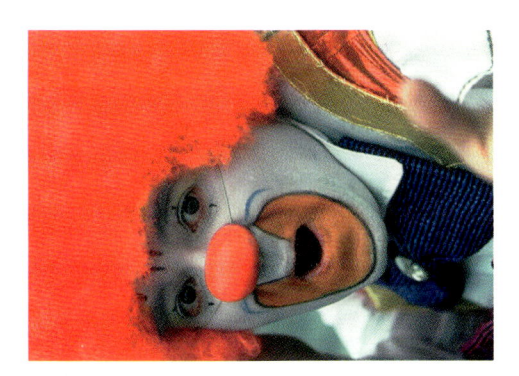

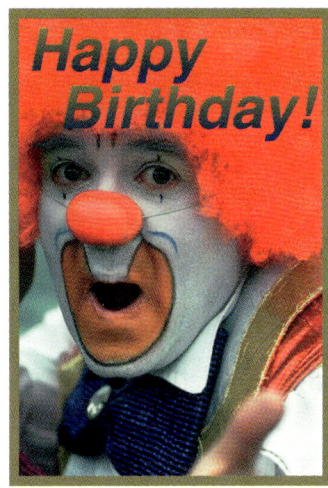

Adding text to an image not only conveys important information, it can also add to the design and overall impact of the image. There are an almost endless variety of typefaces you can use, and text colors can vary from simple black type to the multicolored type shown in this example. You can also fill text with patterns or show photos through the text outlines.

For most of your projects, creating the text in Adobe PhotoDeluxe works just fine. Adobe PhotoDeluxe includes twelve different fonts, but you can use any font that is installed on your computer. To get smooth, legible type in Adobe PhotoDeluxe, you should use TrueType fonts or PostScript fonts with Adobe Type Manager (ATM). A copy of Adobe Type Manager is installed when you install Adobe PhotoDeluxe. You should also be sure that the Anti-Aliased option is always selected in the Type dialog box.

If you're creating very small type, printing at a very high resolution, or enlarging the photo, you might want to create the text in an illustration program such as Adobe Illustrator. Text created in these programs holds its crisp, clean lines no matter how it's scaled. Adobe PhotoDeluxe type, which is created on a grid, can appear jagged and lose detail if it's scanned or created at a low resolution and then printed at a high resolution.

In this technique the text is filled with a gradient. The gradient works particularly well against the solid, bold red of the clown's hair. When adding text, be sure to place it against a background that emphasizes rather than overwhelms it.

1 Open and edit the background for the text

Open the photo you're going to use behind the text. If you're using multiple photos, edit and combine them before adding the text.

In this example the background uses a single, edited photo, which was scanned in a horizontal orientation. To use the photo on a card or poster, such as the invitation created here, it must be switched to a vertical orientation. As a final editing touch, a wide border was added to create a framed look.

Click Get Photo>Open Photo to open the file.

If you want to change the orientation, click Modify>Orientation and then click an orientation button—Rotate Right, Rotate Left, or Free Rotate (rotate to an arbitrary angle). You can also flip a photo horizontally or vertically. This photo was rotated to the right. (It may take Adobe PhotoDeluxe a few seconds to change the orientation. In that case, a progress box appears on the screen.)

To add a border, click Modify>Effects>Outline.

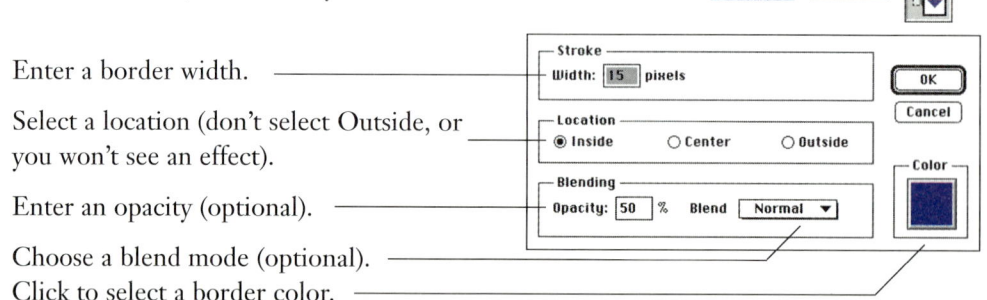

Enter a border width.

Select a location (don't select Outside, or you won't see an effect).

Enter an opacity (optional).

Choose a blend mode (optional).

Click to select a border color.

Click OK to create the border.

The modes in the Outline dialog box are the same as the blends you can set for layers. See "Using blend modes" on page 51 for more information.

Opacity 50%   Opacity 100%

Filling text 79

2 Create the text

Because text in an image must compete with the photo, it's often a good idea to add a little something to emphasize the text. In this technique the text is placed on two lines, filled with a gradient, and resized. Each line of text is created separately.

Click Modify>Tools>Text.

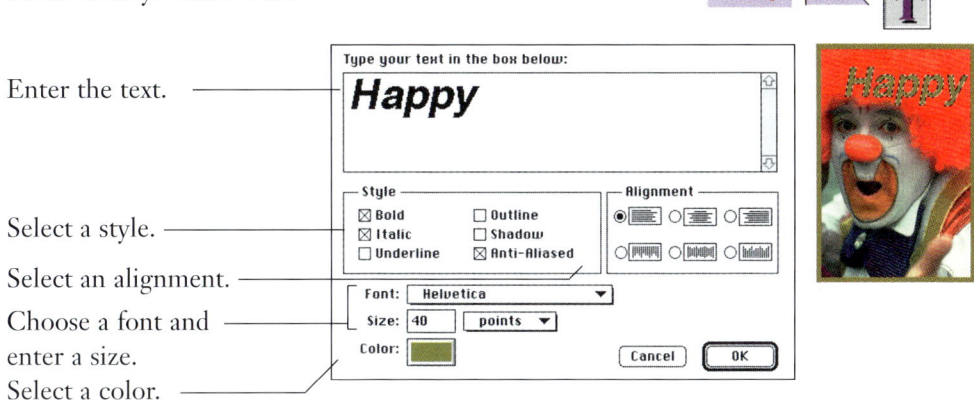

Enter the text.

Select a style.

Select an alignment.

Choose a font and enter a size.

Select a color.

Click OK to add the text.

The text appears as a selection in the photo and a Text layers appears in the Layers palette.

3 Fill the text with a gradient

As long as the text is a selection (it still has its dotted-line border), you can fill it and resize it. A gradient fill starts with one color and gradually moves to another color. You choose the colors and the direction for the fill.

Click Modify>Effects>Gradient Fill.

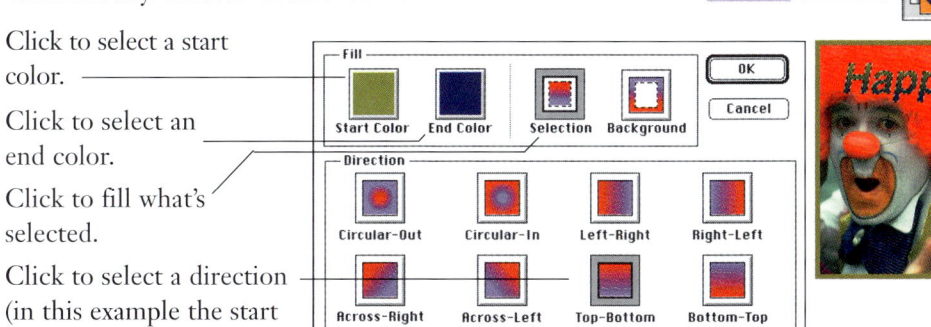

Click to select a start color.

Click to select an end color.

Click to fill what's selected.

Click to select a direction (in this example the start color appears at the top of the selection and the end color appears at the bottom of the selection).

Click OK to fill with the gradient.

4 Resize the text

In this example the text is a too wide to fit across the photo. Separating the text into two lines helps, but the text would look better if it were a little thinner.

Click Modify>Size>Resize. (Resize keeps the same proportions as it changes the selection size.)

Drag a handle to change the height and width.

Click inside the selection with the OK cursor to resize, or click outside the selection with the cancel cursor to try again.

Drag the text into position. Click None to see the text without the selection border.

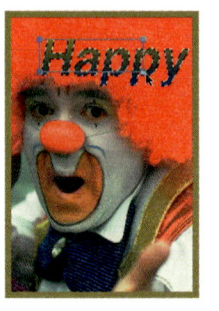

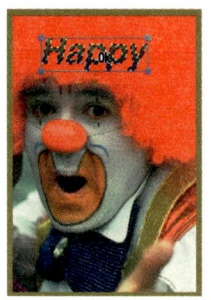

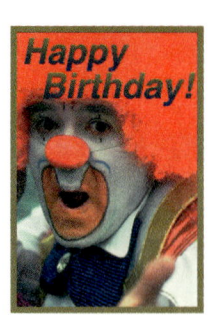

Repeat steps 2, 3, and 4 for each line of text you want to enter.

5 Save the photo

Click Save/Print>Save>Save.

You're ready to print the photo, save it as an Acrobat file, save it in a slide show, or export it into another format to send it via e-mail or display it on the Internet or your personal Web page.

Filling text 81

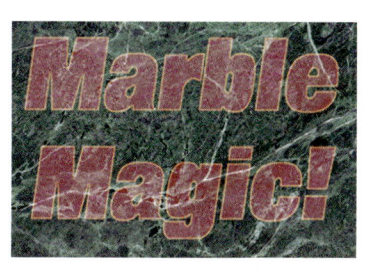

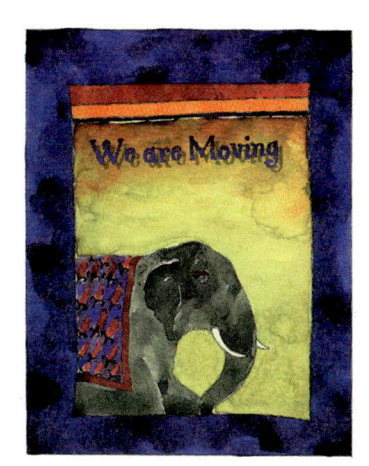

6 Variations

You can move text at any time as long as it's still on a separate layer. If the text is selected, drag the selection. If the text is deselected, use the Move tool to drag the layer.

Balancing color

No matter how carefully they're preserved (and lets face it, most of us archive our photos by tossing them in a drawer), photos fade. The ultraviolet rays of the sun, the instability of photographic paper and chemicals, the acid from black album pages—all of these can cause pictures to lose their original color. Older photos tend to turn yellow; newer photos lose their red and green tones and turn blue.

Rebalancing the color can bring back or even improve on the original color in a photo. As in many restorations, however, the purpose is to make the image look realistic. Old photos, particularly those that were hand-tinted, use subtle, pastel colors for clothes and faces. You can easily reproduce this effect in Adobe PhotoDeluxe.

This technique uses a three-step procedure to correct color:

- Adjust the shadows and highlights
- Color-correct individual areas
- Balance the overall color

Sometimes correcting one color throws another color off balance or removes some of a color's intensity. When you're rebalancing color, it's a game of give and take. You need to experiment with settings until you get the color you like. In this example the photo was adjusted to remove the yellow color cast, then the grass was made greener. Finally, the bloom was put back in Grandpa's and Billy's cheeks.

Balancing color

1 Open the photo and adjust the blacks and whites

Click Get Photo>Open File and open the photo you want to color correct.

Click Modify>Quality>Instant Fix to adjust the blacks (shadows) and whites (highlights).

In order for the other colors to pop into place, a photo needs pure blacks and pure whites. When you use Instant Fix, Adobe PhotoDeluxe automatically searches your photo for the darkest and lightest areas and converts them to black and white. This improves the **contrast** of the photo. Many photos regain their color balance with just this one correction.

Blacks and whites adjusted

2 Select individual areas for correction

Some photos need a little more work to get a good color balance. That's when you start adjusting individual areas. Sometimes Instant Fix removes a color cast from a photo but leaves the rest of the photo looking rather monochromatic. You can dramatically improve a photo by adjusting the hue and saturation of specific colors. To get the final image you want, you might need to adjust the hue and saturation of several individual areas. In this photo, the grass was selected.

The grass is an irregular shape and not a simple selection. First the Rectangle tool was used to select large overlapping areas.

Then the Trace tool was used to add and reduce the selected areas, to achieve a precise outline of the body and clean edges where the grass meets the trees.

3. Change the hue and saturation

Hue refers to the name of a color—blue, green, red, and so on. **Saturation** refers to the strength or purity of the color—for example, deep red or pale blue. If a color has no saturation, it is gray. **Lightness,** a third component of color, refers to the darkness or lightness of the color—for example, dark purple or light orange. In this example the grass was made greener.

Click Modify>Quality>Hue/Saturation.

Drag the slider to change the color.
Drag the slider to change the intensity.

Click OK to change the colors.

Before hue and saturation change

After hue and saturation change

4. Adjust the color balance

The color balance indicates how colors go together. Adding more of one color takes away from another color. Once the hue and saturation in this photo were changed, the faces seemed cold. To correct these tones, the selection was inverted to select the faces and then the color balance was adjusted. To make the flesh tones warmer, some magenta was added to the color balance. (Or, since magenta and green are **complementary colors,** some green was removed to add more magenta to the balance.)

Click Modify>Quality>Color Balance.

Drag the sliders to change the balance.
Click OK to adjust the color balance.

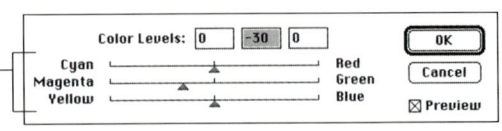

Balancing color   85

This adjustment results in a fairly good color balance, but in making the skin warmer, some of the green in the tree was lost. This could be corrected by selecting the tree and adjusting the color balance again. In this example another solution was used—the photo was trimmed to deemphasize the tree and focus on the people.

Before color balance change

After color balance change

Photo trimmed

5 Save the photo

Click Save/Print>Save>Save.

You're ready to print the photo, save it as an Acrobat file, save it in a slide show, or export it into another format to send it via e-mail or display it on the Internet or your personal Web page.

6 Variations

Sharpening an old photo before you correct the color often improves its quality.

You can also use Hue/Saturation and Color Balance to add color to black-and-white photos. Just select the area you want to color, click the button, and drag the sliders.

The hue settings are based on the location of colors in the standard color wheel. The hue changes according to the direction you would drag to get to a new color. To move clockwise on the wheel, you enter a negative number. To move counter-clockwise, you enter a positive number.

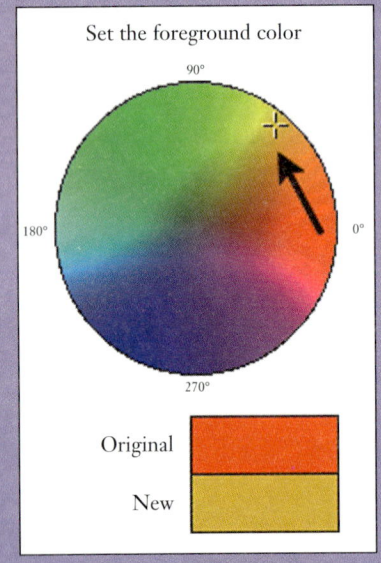

Set the foreground color

90°
180°   0°
270°

Original
New

A value of +50 was entered (move counterclockwise)

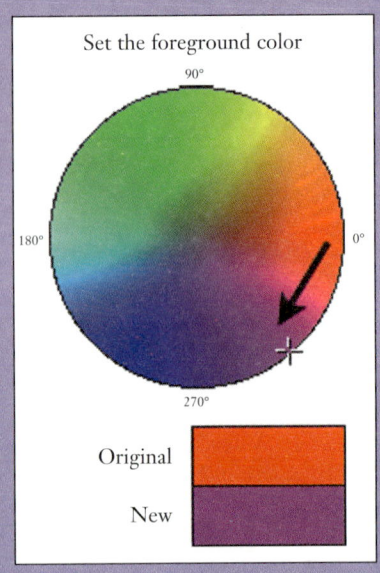

Set the foreground color

90°
180°   0°
270°

Original
New

A value of -50 was entered (move clockwise)

Changing brightness and contrast

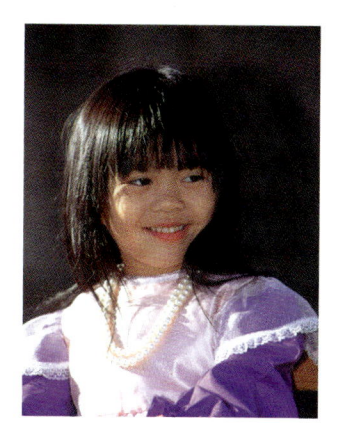

You probably have a great collection of if-only pictures. "If only those people hadn't walked behind me just then. If only that telephone pole wasn't growing out of Jason's head... If only that sunspot hadn't burned the corner of the photo." With Adobe PhotoDeluxe, your if-onlys are a thing of the past. You can transform them into the beautiful photos you imagined them to be.

One common type of if-only is the photo that looks fairly good but lacks contrast. Contrast is the difference between the light and dark parts of a photo. In some cases low contrast makes an entire picture murky. Photos can also lack contrast in specific areas.

If-only photos can also result from of a lack of definition between foreground and background. By diffusing the background, you can improve the photo and direct the viewer's eye to the main subject.

The photo used in this technique is quite appealing in its original form—if only the difference between the background and the child's hair were more distinct, and if only the dress were not quite so bright. One solution to the first problem would be to improve the contrast by filling the background with a lighter color. In this technique a different approach was used. The contrast and brightness of the background were increased, and special effects were used to turn the shadows into a subtle, dreamy pattern. To correct the second problem, the brightest part of the dress was toned down to focus attention on the child's face.

Everyday Uses

1 Open the photo and select the area you want to correct

If your photo is gray, you might want to adjust the contrast and brightness in the entire photo. In this example the background contrast was adjusted.

Click Get Photo>Open Photo to open the photo.

To select an area for correction, click Modify and then choose a selection tool from the pop-up menu in the Select palette. Because the background in this example is one color, a single click of the Color Wand was enough to select the entire background.

2 Increase the brightness and contrast

With Adobe PhotoDeluxe you can adjust both **brightness** (how dull or brilliant the colors are) and **contrast** (the difference between light and dark colors) in a single dialog box.

Click Modify>Quality>Brightness/Contrast.

Drag the slider to change the brightness.
Drag the slider to change the contrast.
Click OK to change the settings.

In this example both the brightness and the contrast of the background were increased.

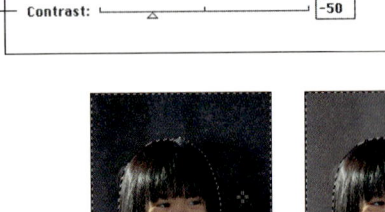

Before brightness and contrast change

After brightness and contrast change

3 Diffuse the background

There are an infinite number of ways to alter a background. Sometimes you might want to make a background less obvious. In this example the background needed to be made more distinct from the foreground. Two special effects were used to enhance this background, posterization and blurring.

Posterization reduces the number of colors in a background. This produces interesting effects in both color and black-and-white photos. Posterization is most effective when you drastically reduce the number of colors (levels) in the photo.

To posterize a selection, click Modify>Effects> Special Effects>Artistic>Posterize.

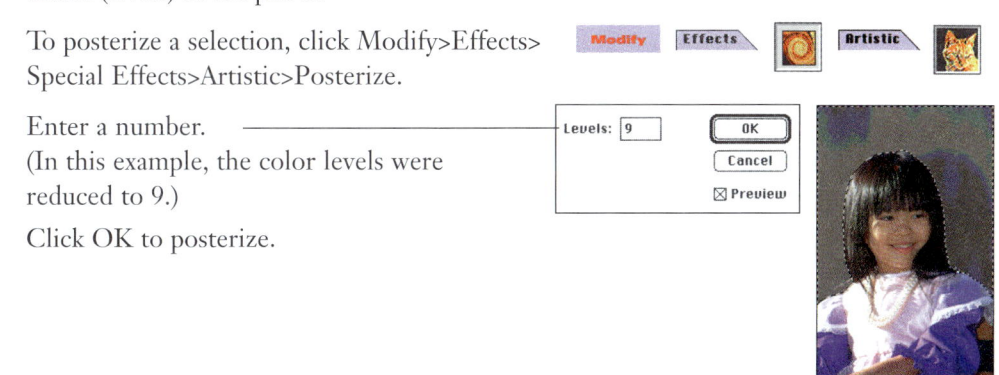

Enter a number.
(In this example, the color levels were reduced to 9.)

Click OK to posterize.

The background was then blurred using the Soften button.

To blur a selection, click Modify>Effects> Special Effects>Blur>Soften.

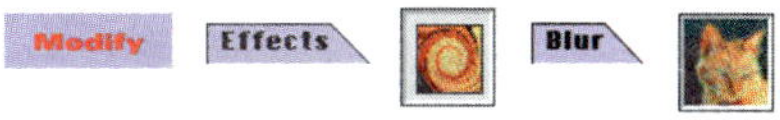

Drag the slider to indicate how much blurring. In this example the blur radius was set to 5. This changed the posterized color into a muted swirl.

Click OK to soften.

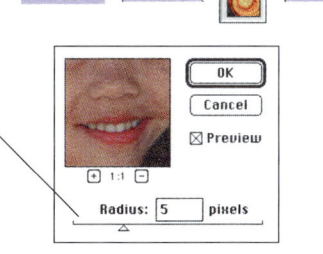

Click Done to leave the Special Effects area.

4 Fine-tune the brightness and contrast

When you adjust one part of a photo, it often changes the overall balance of the picture. With the modifications to the background in this example, the white area in the girl's dress suddenly seemed blinding. As a final touch, the brightness was lowered in just the whitest areas. This unified the picture and put the emphasis back where it belongs—on the sweet face and lovely smile of the child. With a little practice, you'll begin to see what slight changes can do to improve your own photos.

In this example the Color Wand was used to select the whitest area and the brightness was decreased. This final touch gave a better overall balance to the photo.

5 Save the photo

Click Save/Print>Save>Save.

You're ready to print the photo, save it as an Acrobat file, save it in a slide show, or export it into another format to send it via e-mail or display it on the Internet or your personal Web page.

6 Variations

Changing brightness and contrast

Some of the special effect dialog boxes, such as the Soften dialog box, give you two ways to preview an effect. The preview check box shows you the effect in the photo itself. This is the same feature that you find in most dialog boxes.

The small box within the dialog box also shows the preview. This box is useful when you want to preview the effect on a specific part of the photo. When you move the cursor into the box it becomes a hand, and you can drag to see different parts of the photo. To get even more of a close up, you can click the plus box below the window to zoom in on the part of the photo that you want to see.

Sometimes you can't see the effect of a preview on an entire picture because the dialog box covers part of the photo, or you're working in a magnified view of the photo. In this case you can preview the effect on the whole photo by clicking the minus button below the preview window. This zooms out on the preview area. (The actual magnification of the photo window doesn't change).

You might need to be patient while you're waiting for a preview. If displaying the preview will take a few seconds, a flashing line appears under the preview ratio between the Zoom In and Zoom Out buttons.

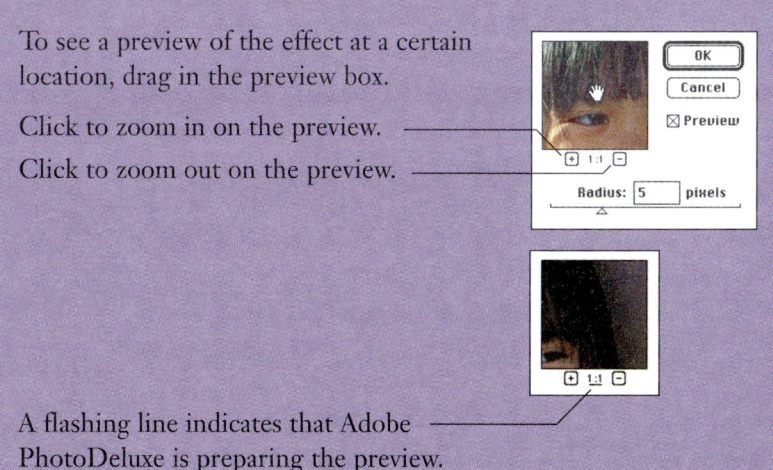

To see a preview of the effect at a certain location, drag in the preview box.

Click to zoom in on the preview.

Click to zoom out on the preview.

A flashing line indicates that Adobe PhotoDeluxe is preparing the preview.

Retouching a face

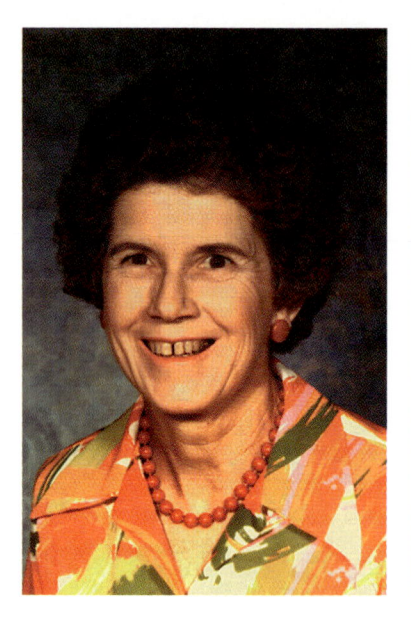

It's axiomatic that the camera can make people look older and heavier, and that harsh lighting has a way of exaggerating wrinkles and flaws. Adobe PhotoDeluxe offers the perfect solution: lighten up, blur, or remove the unflattering areas while accenting the unique characteristics that make the photo appealing.

When retouching a photo, keep in mind that the point is to retouch, not remake! Your goal is a finished photo that looks like the subject, not one that is so perfect it seems artificial. Be subtle. Retouch in small increments and stop frequently to check the overall effect. It can also be helpful to get second opinion.

When working with skin and other areas that have minor color variations, its a good idea to use a **spotting** technique. This method, developed by professional photographers, uses a small brush and a light, translucent ink. An ink color similar to the area to be corrected is mixed and then dabbed on with gentle strokes. The buildup of ink gradually produces the desired color. Spotting keeps corrections from being too noticeable.

In this technique lightening was used to remove the circles under the eyes and spotting was used to remove the wrinkles from the face and neck. The gap between the teeth was filled in using copy and paste. The final photo appears natural and vibrant, sure to please the viewer and the viewed.

Retouching a face

1 Open the photo and remove the shadows

Click Get Photo>Open Photo to open the file.

To remove shadows, you lighten the dark areas using a color that matches the rest of the skin tones. To select shadows, the Color Wand tool usually works best. In this example the shadow colors are only slightly different from the other face tones, so a low tolerance was set for the Color Wand. (See "Selecting by color" on page 14 for information on Color Wand tolerance.)

To lower the Color Wand tolerance, choose File>Preferences>Cursors.

Enter a low value (5 to 15).

Click OK to change the tolerance.

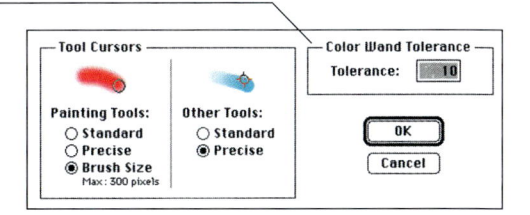

In this example the tolerance was set to 10 and the Add button was selected. Several clicks of the Color Wand were necessary to isolate the darker areas under the eyes.

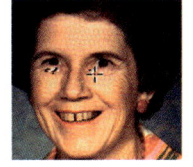

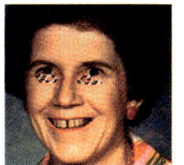

To change the skin color, a flesh tone was selected from the face and the selection was filled with this color. (See "Selecting a color" on page 18 for information about selecting a color from inside a photo.) Lowering the opacity of the fill made the color change less apparent.

Click Modify>Effects>Selection Fill.

Enter a low opacity.

Click to select the fill color. (In this example a color near the eyes was selected.)

Click to fill what's selected.

Click OK to change the color.

Once the shadows are filled, click None to see the final result. The change is so subtle you might think nothing has happened. To see the effect more clearly, click Undo repeatedly to toggle between the before and after versions of the photo.

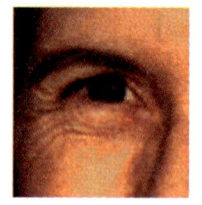

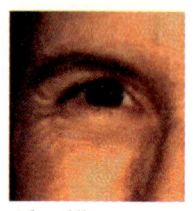

Before fill   After fill

2 Remove the wrinkles

You need patience to remove wrinkles. They took a long time to get there; so give them a little time to go away. The idea is to work in small stages and apply the color gradually. You'll probably need to change the painting color frequently, always selecting a color that's near the tone of the area you're retouching.

Click Modify>Tools>Brush.

Select a fine, soft-edged brush from the Brushes palette. Click the color box and, while the Color Swatches palette is open, select a paint color from the photo.

Dab the color on gently and select new colors as you move from area to area. Zoom in so you can paint with precision and then zoom out to keep tabs on the overall effect. Repeat the process until the wrinkles are gone.

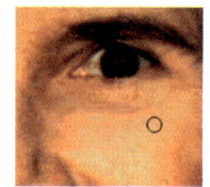

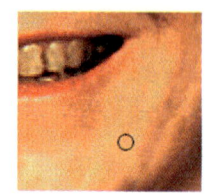

3 Enhance the smile

Retouching teeth can be tricky. Teeth vary in color and shape so much that it's not always easy to get the selection and color you want. You need to be guided by the natural colors and shapes in the original photo. With a little practice, you can effectively whiten yellowed teeth and fill in small gaps.

Retouching a face

Select the teeth you want to correct. In this example the teeth were selected using the Color Wand and Trace tools. The Add and Reduce buttons were used to fine tune the selection.

To whiten teeth, you can fill them using the Lighten blend in the Selection Fill dialog box. Lighten slightly washes out the color. These blends are the same ones you can set for layers. For more information, see "Using blend modes" on page 51.

Click Modify>Effects>Selection Fill.

Enter a low opacity.

Choose Lighten.

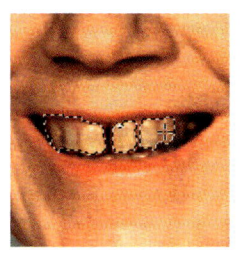

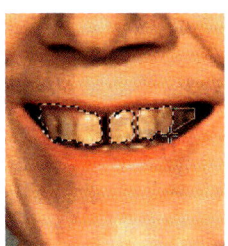

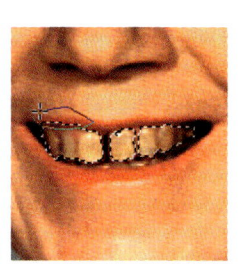

Click to select the fill color (you might want to choose a color from the teeth themselves).

Click to fill what's selected.

Click OK to change the color.

To fill the gap between the teeth, the left tooth was copied and pasted over itself. Then the copied selection was nudged to the right to cover the gap. (To nudge a selection, use the arrow keys on your keyboard.) You can also use this procedures to hide dental fillings.

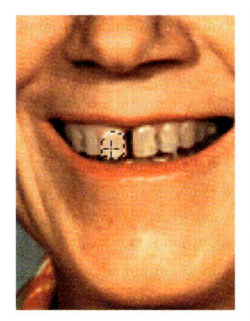

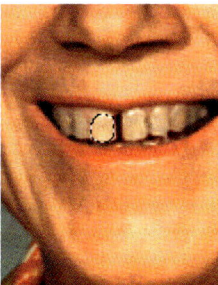

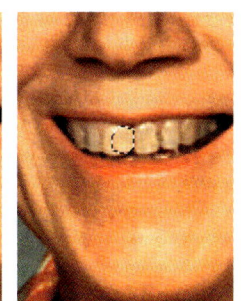

4 Save the photo

Click Save/Print>Save>Save.

You're ready to print the photo, save it as an Acrobat file, save it in a slide show, or export it into another format to send it via e-mail or display it on the Internet or your personal Web page.

5 Variations

Try varying the brush size and hardness to get different retouching effects.

If you need just a slight adjustment to hide a flaw, of if you want to smooth out the edges around corrected areas, click Modify>Tools>Smudge. Drag from the correct color into the area you want to obscure.

To get the soft focus look that is so popular with aging actresses, click Modify>Quality>Effects>Special Effects>Blur>Soften. This effect can help to disguise retouched areas.

Creating a business card

For a small business, one of the most important aspects of advertising is establishing a personal identity. Nothing is more effective in conveying who you are and what you do than a dynamic, powerful business card. The old adage "a picture is worth a thousand words" is especially true when you're advertising a product or service.

When choosing a photo for your card, think about the amount of text you want to add and the balance of the photo with the text. Too much text or too many typefaces can obscure, rather than highlight, your message. Be sure the type is large enough to be read easily.

To make an immediate but long-lasting impression, select or create a simple uncluttered image that has areas of neutral color to serve as a background for the text. For a professional look, consider creating the type in an illustration program such as Adobe Illustrator and then opening the text file in Adobe PhotoDeluxe.

In this example the same font was used for both pieces of text, varying only the capitalization and the font size. Because the picture has quite a bit going on, the visual effect was toned down by lowering the opacity of the photo. This produced a muted effect, while maintaining the action of the photo and its effectiveness as an informative and interesting background.

You'll probably want to take your card to a copy center or service bureau for printing. Most centers have special deals on business packages, and you can often have several hundred cards printed on a thick stock for a very reasonable price. You can also use the same image on your stationery, on flyers, or in a print advertisement.

1 Open the photo and add the text

Click Get Photo>Open Photo to open the file.

When you're adding a lot of text, it's often easier to add the text in two or more stages. This lets you move and size the text pieces independently and to observe how each text entry affects the image as a whole.

Click Modify>Tools>Text.

To enter text on separate lines, press Return at the end of each line. The preview you see in the text box is exactly the way the text will appear in the photo.

Enter the text.

Select a style and alignment.

Choose a font and enter a size.

Click to select a color.

Click OK to add the text.

The text appears in the photo as a selection and a new layer appears in the Layers palette.

Drag to move the text into position. You can also click None to deselect the text (so you can see it without its selection border), and then use the Move tool to drag the Text layer into place.

Click Modify>Tools>Text and enter any additional text. New text is added to the same Text layer. The new text is now the selection, and the the old text is deselected. To move additional text, you must drag the *selection*, since dragging the layer moves all the text.

2 Try out different layer options

To experiment with different looks for the card, you can vary the layer blend and the layer opacity. Changing the blend is especially effective when you have overlying areas of solid color. You must have two or more layers to see any difference in the ways the layers blend together. For more information on blends, see "Using blend modes" on page 51.

In this example, when the blend setting is set to Normal the brown type looks good on the blue sky but doesn't show up very well on the lumber and roof areas. You could change the color of the text, but you can also see how changing the blend setting of the Text layer changes the color of the text. Reducing the opacity of the Photo layer adds "snap" to the text.

To modify a layer's settings, double-click the layer name in the Layers palette.

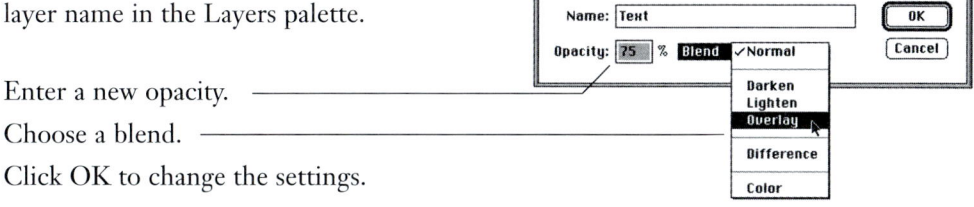

Enter a new opacity.

Choose a blend.

Click OK to change the settings.

Normal blend

Lighten blend

Darken blend

Difference blend

Normal blend, 75% opacity

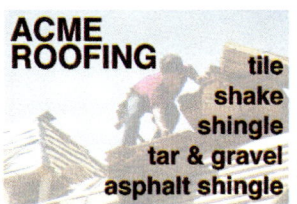

Normal blend, 25% opacity

3 Save the photo

Click Save/Print>Save>Save.

You're ready to print the photo, save it as an Acrobat file, save it in a slide show, or export it into another format to send it via e-mail or display it on the Internet or your personal Web page.

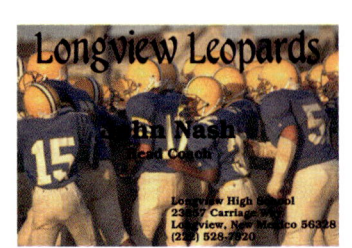

4 Variations

In some cases you might want to add text on separate layers rather than adding multiple text entries to a single layer. For example, you might want to try out different fill colors and positions for each entry independently. To do this, create the first Text layer in the usual way. When the first piece of text is in place, double-click the Text layer and give it a new name. The next time you click the Text tool, Adobe PhotoDeluxe creates a new Text layer.

Several of the Adobe PhotoDeluxe dialog boxes let you quickly revert to previous settings without leaving the dialog box. To undo an entry, press the Option key. The Cancel button becomes the Reset button and you can click Reset to return to the former settings.

Click to cancel

Press Option and click to reset

Filling selections

Adobe PhotoDeluxe is the perfect companion for armchair decorators. Now, without getting up, you can redo the bathroom, change the wallpaper in the living room, or even do an entire exterior paint job. When it comes time to actually do the work, you'll have a clear and exact picture of what you want to do. Using Adobe PhotoDeluxe to try out different looks can save you time, money, and energy. Here's your chance to experiment with weird colors and wild patterns, before you invest a single cent or paint a single stroke.

To change the color of any area in a photo, you select the area and then fill it. Filling is quicker than painting with a brush and lets you choose different opacities and blend modes for the color.

To maintain the texture or detail of the object, fill it with an opacity of less than 100%. In this example the sections of the house were selected and then filled with semitranslucent color.

1 Open the photo and select the areas you want to change

Click Get Photo>Open Photo to open the photo.

To make the selection, click Modify and then choose a selection tool from the pop-up menu on the Select palette.

When you're changing the color of a solid-colored area, it's easiest to select the area using the Color Wand tool. If you're selecting several areas, make sure the Add button is selected before you select multiple areas.

In this example the Color Wand tool was used to select the individual gray areas. Because some of the areas of the house are in shadow, the Color Wand did not make a perfect selection (the shadow areas fell outside of the tolerance set for the Color Wand). These areas were filled in later.

2 Create a painting layer and fill the selection

Filling on a separate layer keeps the original photo intact. Click the New button in the Layers palette to create the layer and set the layer options.

In this example the layer opacity was set to 50% and the layer blend was set to Darken.

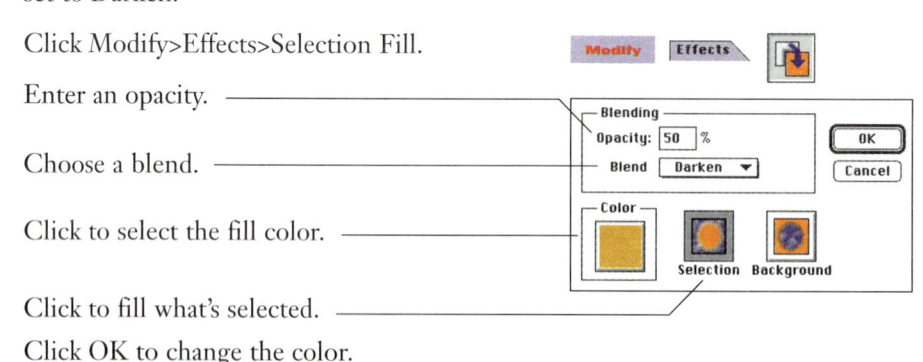

Click Modify>Effects>Selection Fill.

Enter an opacity.

Choose a blend.

Click to select the fill color.

Click to fill what's selected.

Click OK to change the color.

Filling selections

The opacity (50%) and blend setting (Darken) of the layer produced a muted color and allowed the texture of the siding to show through.

3 Clean up the paint job

To touch up the areas that are not filled, you must first deselect. (As long as there is a selection, you can't paint outside the selection border.) Click None in the Select palette to deselect.

To paint the small areas, click Modify>Tool>Brush and select a small brush. In this example a fill color was chosen from the photo. When you're painting small areas, you should zoom in and paint with small strokes so you can easily undo.

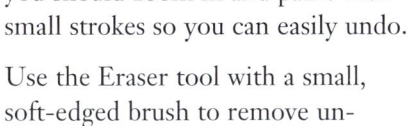

Use the Eraser tool with a small, soft-edged brush to remove unwanted color from the photo.

4 Save the photo

Click Save/Print>Save>Save.

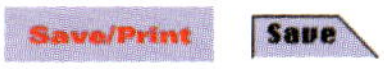

You're ready to print the photo, save it as an Acrobat file, save it in a slide show, or export it into another format to send it via e-mail or display it on the Internet or your personal Web page.

5 Variations

If you're filling something and you want it to have very soft edges (more than you can accomplish with the soft-edged brushes), click Modify>Effects>Feather and enter a pixel value to increase the soft edges.

There are two ways to change the opacity and blend of a fill. If you want to set the same opacity and blend for all the selections you're changing, you can create a layer and set the layer opacity and blend. This is the method used in this technique.

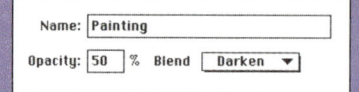

Filling selections

You can also change the opacity and blend for each selection individually. When you want selections to have different opacities and blends, you keep the layer opacity at 100% and the layer blend set to Normal. You then change the settings in the Selection Fill dialog box as you fill each selection.

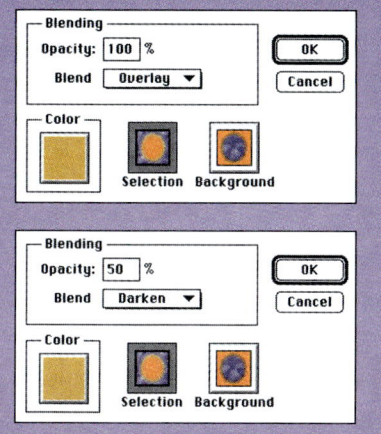

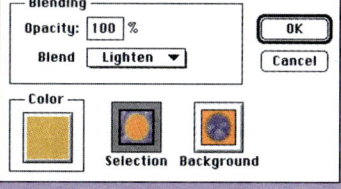

All of these selection are on the same layer and filled with the same color. The settings in the Fill Selection were changed for each selection.

100% Overlay

100% Normal

50% Darken

100% Lighten

Creating a panorama

Whatever the reason—the fear of missing the peak moment of a great sunset, the security of needing a backup shot, the overwhelming beauty of the mountains—you often return from a trip with many, many, many similar photos. Perhaps you purposely shot a 360° because you wanted to capture it all. Intentional or not, you can often combine two or more ho-hum photos into a spectacular panorama.

To be used together, the photos must be from approximately the same distance and perspective and have similar color balance and contrast. It's possible to cut out parts of photos that are flawed when you're combining them. Consider scanning in only the sections you're going to use. This helps keep down the file size of each photo.

The most challenging part of creating a panorama is overlapping the photos and lining up the edges. Have you ever tried doing this with ordinary photos? It's nerve-wracking—especially when you can't keep the photos in place as you try to tape the backs, or you cut the photos to fit before you realize you have the end images switched. By using Adobe PhotoDeluxe layers to overlap the images, you can be sure you have the effect you want before you do anything final. If your photos are small, you can combine three or more images. The main limitation to the number of photos is the size of the photo files and the size of the final panorama file.

This technique combines two photos, adjusting the brightness and contrast of the images to make the final photo consistent in color and tone.

1 Store all but one of the photos in the Hold Folder

Before you begin the panorama, decide which of the photos will be your starting point. Then open each of the other photos you're using and save them in the Hold Photo folder. In this example the mountain landscape was the starting image, so the photo of the hiker was put into the Hold Photo folder.

Click Get Photo>Open Photo to open the first photo.

Click Save/Print>Save>Hold Photo Folder to save the photo in the Hold Photo folder.

Repeat this step for each photo you're using in the panorama.

2 Open the starting photo and increase the canvas

With the photos stored in Hold Photo, you're ready to create the composite photo. Your first step is to open the starting file and increase the file's dimensions, so that the file can accommodate the photos you're adding. Be sure to leave a little room for overlap (you'll need it for positioning). It's easy to trim the photo when you're finished.

Click Get Photo>Open Photo to open the starting photo.

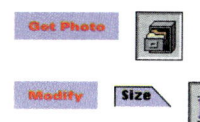

Click Modify>Size>Canvas Size.

Enter new dimensions. (In this example, the width was increased by 4 inches and the height was increased by 1.5 inches.)

Click where you want the photo to appear in relation to the new canvas. (In this example the photo was placed in the middle left portion of the new canvas)

Resize the window so that you can see as much of it as possible. If you have a small monitor, you'll probably have to scroll as you edit the panorama.

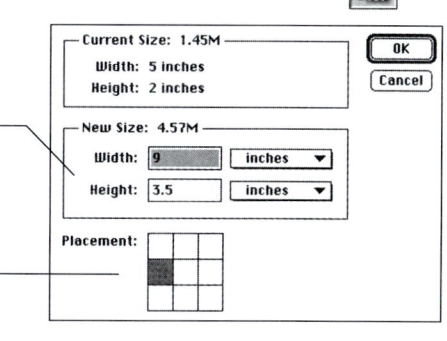

3 Get the photo from the Hold Photo folder and line up the photos

When you drag a photo from the Hold Photo folder, Adobe PhotoDeluxe automatically makes a new layer. To be able to see through the photo as you adjust its position, make the layer less than 100% opacity. You can restore the opacity after you've got the second photo in place.

Click the Hold Photo bar.

The contents of the Hold Photo folder appear in a window. Move the photo to the open window (you can double-click the photo, drag the photo, or select the photo and click Paste Layer). The Make Layer dialog box appears.

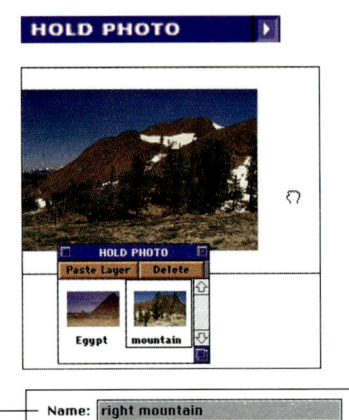

Enter a name.

Enter an opacity of less than 100%.

Click OK to create the layer.

The second photo appears in the middle of the window, overlapping part of the first photo.

Use the Move tool to drag the second photo close to its final position.

Repeat this procedure until all the photos are in the file and near their final locations.

4 Make final adjustments

To make the final adjustments, you need to see the photos at full opacity. In the Layers palette, double-click the name of the layer you're positioning. Enter an opacity of 100% in the Layer Options dialog box and then click OK.

Use the arrow keys on the keyboard to move the photo in small increments until it's in position.

In this example once the two photos were placed side by side it was easy to see the difference in brightness and size. Your photo may also need contrast or color adjustment.

To adjust brightness or contrast, click Modify>Quality> Brightness/Contrast.

To match these photos, the brightness was decreased in the second photo.

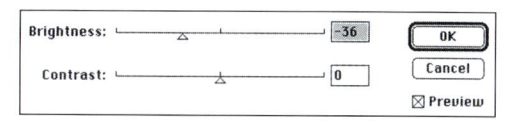

To adjust color in the photos, click Modify>Quality. In most cases you can match the color using the Instant Fix button. If your photos need more correction, use the Color Balance or Hue/Saturation button.

> If fine lines are still visible after you've adjusted the photos, click Modify>Tools>Smudge and use a soft-edged brush to dab along the seams in the photo.

As a final adjustment, the photos used in this example needed to be trimmed. Merge the layers before you trim them. To delete a layer, click the Delete button in the Layers palette. Select Merge Visible Layers in the dialog box and click OK.

To trim a photo, click Modify>Size>Trim.

Drag to select the area *you want to keep*, then click inside the box. To cancel the trim, click outside the box and then drag again.

5 Save the photo

Click Save/Print>Save>Save.

You're ready to print the photo, save it as an Acrobat file, save it in a slide show, or export it into another format to send it via e-mail or display it on the Internet or your personal Web page.

6 Variations

Perform daring feats of engineering

> To avoid opening and then saving files in Adobe PhotoDeluxe, you can drag files into the Hold Folder when you're in the Finder. To be recognized by Adobe PhotoDeluxe, however, the files must be in either Adobe PhotoDeluxe or Photoshop format. Photos in other file formats won't appear when you open the Hold Folder window.

> To save disk space, you should empty the Hold Photo folder when you're finished working with the photos. If you've created the file in Adobe PhotoDeluxe and stored it only in the Hold Photo folder, be sure to save a copy on your hard disk before you delete. To delete the photos, select them in the Hold Photo window and click Delete, or open the Hold folder in the Finder and drag the files to the Trash.

Using layers to try out effects

Very few people are satisfied with the hair color they were born with. As teenagers, everyone wonders what they'd look like with longer or shorter hair, curly or straight hair, blond or brunette hair—or green or purple hair! When they get older, people try to remember what color their hair was, or even when they had any hair at all. Adobe PhotoDeluxe can't do anything about your genetic heritage, but it can help you change your photographic image.

Whether you want to alter your eyes, your hair, your clothes, or your location, the basic technique is the same. You select what you want to change and then fill, paint, or paste something different into the selection. Most of the fun in experimenting is combining several possibilities, so your best bet is to put the fill for each selection on a separate layer. Then you can try out lots of different looks by turning the layers on and off.

In this example the varying hair colors and dress colors were mixed and matched. The final result turned this rather prim and sedate young lady into a punk groupie wannabe. (For something completely different, try adding grunge clothes, four or five earrings, and a check tattoo to your favorite teenager's photo.)

Everyday Uses

1 Open the photo and select the areas you want to change

Click Get Photo>Open Photo to open the photo.

To make the selection, click Modify and then choose a selection tool from the pop-up menu in the Select palette.

To change clothes, you would probably use the Trace tool to select the body. To change eye color, you might use the Color Wand in conjunction with the Trace tool.

In this example the hair is made up of various shades, but to the Color Wand tool these colors are similar to the background colors. To make this selection easier the Color Wand tolerance was lowered to 20, so that each click of the Color Wand selected a precise color. For more information about setting tolerance, see "Selecting by color" on page 14.

2 Create a new layer and fill the selection

Filling the same selection on several layers lets you keep your choices open. Click New in the Layers palette to create a layer and set the layer options, then fill the selection.

Click Modify>Effects>Selection Fill.

Enter an opacity.
Choose a blend.
Click to select the fill color.
Click to fill what's selected.
Click OK to change the color.

To avoid a "painted" look, fill the selection with less than 100% opacity, so that some texture shows through the fill. You can set the opacity in the Layers dialog box when you create the layer, or in the Selection Fill dialog box when you fill the selection.

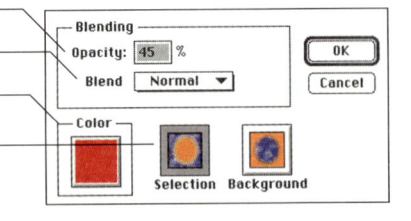

Filled at 100% opacity   Filled at 45% opacity

Using layers to try out effects 113

You can also use a different blend for each layer. See "Using blend modes" on page 51 for more information on setting blends for layers.

To fill a selection with a blend, choose the blend in the Fill Selection dialog box. See "Filling selections" on page 101 for information on setting individual selection blends.

3 Fill the selection on several layers

You might not always be happy with your first color change. Well, here's where the power of layers comes in. You can try out a different color without letting go of your first choice. Repeat the fill procedure on another layer or two.

In this example the hair was filled with purple at an opacity of 45%. Although the opacity of the red and purple fills is the same, the hair looks more opaque in this image. That's because the red and purple layers are combined. Whenever more than one layer is visible, you're looking at the mixture of all the colors and opacities from each layer.

To see how the Purple layer looks by itself, you can turn off the Red layer. To make a layer invisible, click the eye icon next to the layer name in the Layers palette. Click again to turn the layer back on.

4 Experiment with other layers

With the hair's vibrant new color, the dress seemed rather drab in comparison. You'll probably find in your own projects that changing one selection gives you ideas about modifying other parts of the photo.

To try out some livelier dress colors in this example, Layer 0 was activated (the other layers contain only hair colors) and the dress was selected using the Color Wand tool.

Several layers were created to try out dress colors. The dress was pasted on each layer and filled with a different color.

You can only have six layers at a time, so you may find that you have to delete a layer or merge layers as you go along. Click the Delete button in the Layers palette to delete or merge layers. For more information, see "Merging layers" on page 24.

Turn the layers on and off in the Layers palette to see all the possible combinations.

5 Save the photo

Click Save/Print>Save>Save.

You're ready to print the photo, save it as an Acrobat file, save it in a slide show, or export it into another format to send it via e-mail or display it on the Internet or your personal Web page.

6 Variations

Using layers to try out effects 115

When you're using the Color Wand tool, where you click can make a big difference. As an alternative to changing the Color Wand tolerance, try clicking a color, undoing if not enough or too much is selected, and then clicking a different spot.

You may find that after you've merged layers there are a few areas that need to be touched up. You'll probably have to blend the edges between filled areas or add small amounts of color to unfilled areas. To touch up the photo, click Modify>Tools> Smudge. Use a small, soft-edged brush to blend the colors.

Because Adobe PhotoDeluxe can have only one selection at a time, filling selections on separate layers is a roundabout way of storing a selection (that is, a shape). To reselect a shape, you can return to any filled layer and use the Color Wand tool to select the transparent areas. Invert the selection to return to the former selection. For example, suppose you were working on the dress selection but decided you want to try out yet another hair color. You could activate one of the hair color layers, select the transparent areas, invert the selection, and then create a new layer and fill the selection.

Original layer   Transparency selected   Selection inverted   New layer created and filled

Color correcting a landscape

Sometimes when you're on vacation, especially when you're in a beautiful natural hideaway, what you experience is not what you get on film. How many times have you eagerly awaited your vacation photos, only to find when they came back that the sky was really quite cloudy, or a haze obscured the distant mountains, or a fog hid the ocean's horizon? Using Adobe PhotoDeluxe, you can make your pictures reflect your memories. (This is a perfectly legal way to alter your reality!)

Touching up a landscape is similar to touching up a face or a body—if you go overboard the photo looks artificial and phony. In the real world the sky is rarely a solid Kodachrome blue or the ocean a continuous aquamarine. To bring some of nature's variation back into the scene, you can fill landscape areas with a gradient instead of solid color. (A gradient fill starts with one color and gradually fades into a second color.) This avoids the travel brochure look, while still creating the photo you wish you'd gotten.

In this example the color was modified to make the trees greener and then the sky was filled with a blue gradient, producing a much warmer, sunnier photo.

Color correcting a landscape 117

1 Open the photo and correct the color balance

> When you're making color corrections, it's a good idea to start with corrections that affect the entire photo and then move on to specific areas.

In this example the color balance is not too bad, but the trees are dark and muddy. To brighten the trees, more green was added to the image.

Click Get Photo>Open Photo to open the photo.

To balance the color, click Modify>Quality>Color Balance.

Drag toward the color you want to add.

Click OK to change the color balance.

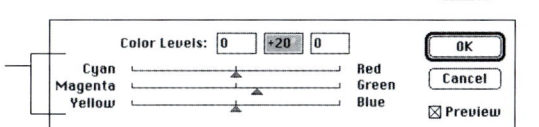

Correcting color balance requires some experimenting because correcting one color always has an effect on the other colors. When you're correcting overall balance, focus on one color that you want to correct and drag the sliders to adjust that color.

As green was added to this photo, the trees were used as the color gauge. (The amount of green used washed out the background, but this was later corrected with the gradient fill.)

Your photos will need different color corrections. If the photo is too dark or too light, try using Instant Fix. To add contrast, use Contrast/Brightness. If the photo has a definite color cast, such as the blue tint often found in faded color photos, try using Color Balance to remove the tint. As you work with your photos, you'll get a feel for which type of color correction works best in specific situations.

2 Correct individual selections

There are several ways to correct individual areas in a landscape. You can paint, fill, or even copy and paste from other parts of the same photo or from other pictures. Whatever method you use, remember to keep the colors as natural as possible.

In this example the washed-out sky was turned into a brilliant blue. In nature, skies are not a solid, continuous color. In the uncorrected photo, for example, the sky has many colors and variations. To keep this effect in the corrected photo, the sky was filled with a gradient.

First the sky was selected using the Color Wand tool. Then the selection was filled with a gradient that uses two shades of blue.

To fill with a gradient, click Modify>Effects>Gradient Fill.

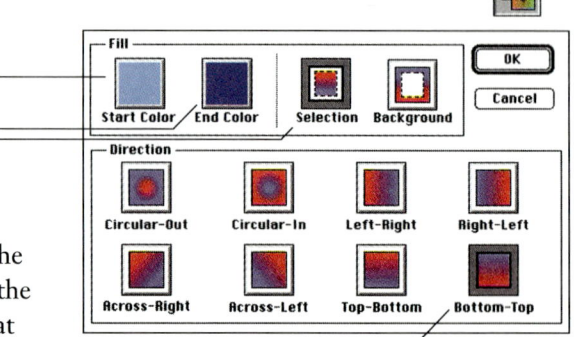

Click to select a start color.

Click to select an end color.

Click to fill what's selected.

Select a direction. (In this example the start color appears at the bottom of the selection and the end color appears at top of the selection.)

Click OK to fill with the gradient.

Color correcting a landscape 119

Click None in the Select palette to see the finished landscape.

That's all the correction that this photo needed. Repeat this selection and correction process until your photo looks just the way you want it.

3 Save the photo

Click Save/Print>Save>Save.

You're ready to print the photo, save it as an Acrobat file, save it in a slide show, or export it into another format to send it via e-mail or display it on the Internet or your personal Web page.

4 Variations

If you want a "picture-perfect" sky, click Modify>Effects>Fill and select a medium blue for the sky. This solid color makes the mountains look like the two-dimensional cutouts used in old westerns.

Even when you fill with a gradient, the color may still look too even. You can "dirty up" any selection by adding a small amount of noise. To add noise, click Modify>Effects>Special Effects>Blur>Noise.

The sliders in the Color Balance dialog box work on the principle of complementary colors. Imagine all the primary colors arranged in a circle, equidistant from each other. Each color is directly opposite from its complement, and each color is between the two colors used to create it. For example, adding yellow and cyan produces green; therefore green in located on the color wheel between yellow and cyan.

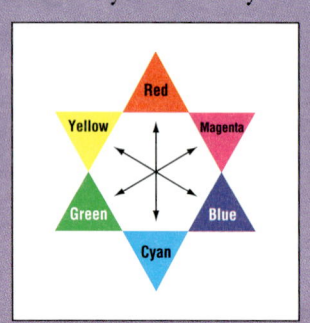

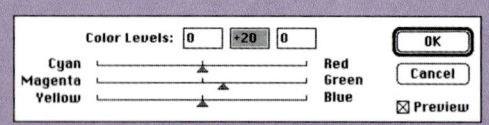

When you drag the sliders in the Color Balance dialog box, you're moving between complementary colors. To add color to a photo, you subtract its complement (the color opposite it on the wheel). For example, to increase the green in an image, you decrease the magenta. Understanding this relationship between colors helps you predict what will happen when you drag one of the sliders in the Color Balance dialog box.

Using the scanner as a camera

Scanning turns your photos into digital images. Whether you scan them yourself, have them scanned at a copy center, or get your processed photos back on a CD-ROM or floppy disk, the prints or negatives have been scanned somewhere along the line. See "Getting photos into Adobe PhotoDeluxe" on page 5 for more information on scanning.

If you have your own scanner you don't have to limit its use to scanning photos. You can use your scanner as a digital camera and to scan in all kinds of objects—leaves, keys, fabric, toys, coins, and perhaps most fun of all, body parts.

Scanners are made to scan flat surfaces, so you have to use a little ingenuity to scan in three-dimensional objects. The important thing is to keep any ambient light from hitting the scanner bed as the scan is being made. Otherwise you'll have streaks and shadows in the scan. To scan a bulky object, lay the object on the scanning surface and then cover it with a towel or other heavy material. Hold down the top of the scanner as you scan (if you're scanning your own body, you'll need some help).

In this example a hand was placed on the scanner. Then a photo was combined with the scan to make these animated finger puppets.

121

Everyday Uses

1 Store any additional photos in the Hold Photo folder

If you're going to combine photos for the final image, open and store the photos you'll need in the Hold Photo folder. You can make editing changes before or after you store the photos.

Click Get Photo>Open Photo to open the photo.

Click Save/Print>Save>Hold Photo to store the photo.

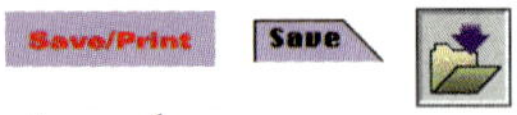

In this example the editing changes needed to blend the women into the fingers were made after the photos were combined.

2 Combine the photos

Click Get Photo>Open Photo to open the photo you're using as the starting point of the image.

To retrieve a photo, click the Hold Photo bar.

The contents of the Hold Photo folder appear in a window under the open photo. Move the photo to the open window. (You can double-click the photo, drag the photo, or select the photo and then click Paste Layer.)

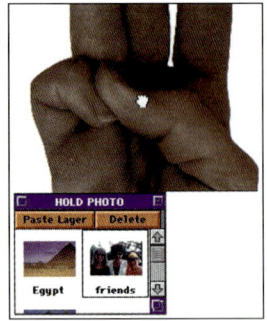

When you drag a photo from the Hold Photo folder, Adobe PhotoDeluxe automatically makes a new layer and displays the Make Layer dialog box. Name the layer and enter an opacity of less than 100%, so you can "see through" the top photo to position it on the bottom photo.

Enter a name.

Enter an opacity of less than 100%.

Click OK to create the layer.

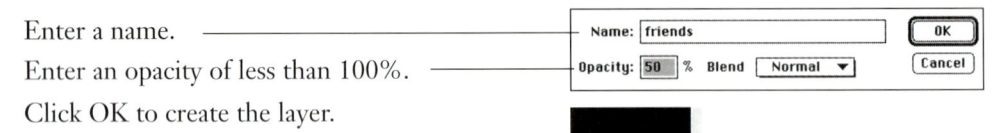

Using the scanner as a camera 123

The photo from the Hold Photo folder appears in the middle of the window.

Use the Move tool to drag the photo into position. The top photo is easy to place because it's not opaque. As long as a photo is on its own layer, you can move it as much as you want without affecting the bottom photo.

3 Edit the image

You may need to edit your image to remove the unwanted parts of the photo you pasted in. Before editing, select the layer you want to edit in the Layers palette.

In this example much of the photo needed to be removed to leave just the heads. The Eraser tool with a small brush was used to edit the photo.

When you're finished editing, double-click the layer in the Layers palette and then set the layer's opacity to 100% in the Layers Options dialog box.

To smooth the edges between the photos, you can blend the seams using the Smudge tool. Click Modify>Tools>Smudge and select a fine brush from the Smudges palette. Use small strokes to erase any seams in the combined photo.

124   **Everyday Uses**

4 Save the photo

Click Save/Print>Save>Save.

You're ready to print the photo, save it as an Acrobat file, save it in a slide show, or export it into another format to send it via e-mail or display it on the Internet or your personal Web page.

5 Variations

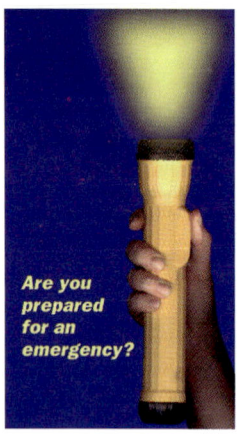

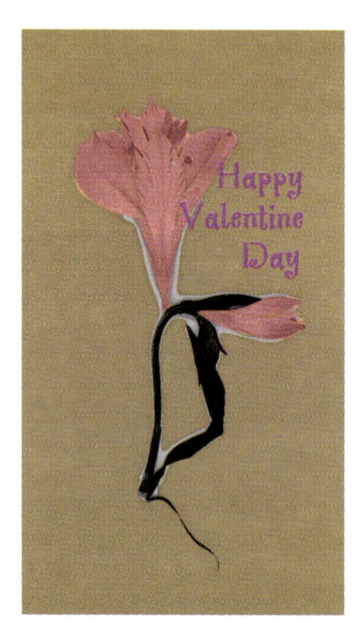

SECTION 4

Special Effects

This section presents techniques that show the real power and muscle of Adobe PhotoDeluxe. Once you graduate to this section, you're ready to move beyond simple substitution and editing into the world of creativity and design.

In this section you'll find out how to jazz up backgrounds with filters, drop shadows, and other special effects. You'll learn how to use Adobe PhotoDeluxe to draw shapes and create abstract patterns and weird textures. And you'll learn how to create text as an integral part of a design instead of an afterthought. You'll even learn how to rid your photos of spurned lovers.

Use these techniques as jumping off points for your own work. There are no rules or limits—experiment and explore and soon even you will be amazed at what you produce!

Adding motion to a photo 126
Drawing a pattern 130
Showing a photo through text 135
Creating backgrounds with filters 140
Combining different types of photos 144
Using text as a background 149
Duplicating, flipping, and rotating selections 154
Creating a kaleidoscope effect 159
Working with a grid 163
Replacing body parts 168
Covering up problem areas 173
Landscaping your yard 178
Creating abstract textures 183
Adding a drop shadow 188
Changing orientation and perspective 193
Creating a complex collage 198
Combining different-sized photos 203
Creating a brochure or report cover 207
Creating cartoons 212
Using hidden bonus filters 217

Adding motion to a photo

How often have you been enticed by a car ad on television that implies you're tearing down a deserted country road at incredibly illegal speeds with your hair flying and the person of your dreams sitting next to you? You can use Adobe PhotoDeluxe to help create your own fantasies of speed and romance, without risking arrest.

To create the illusion of speed or motion in a photo, you use a variation of the panning technique used by sports and nature photographers. When photographing fast-moving athletes or objects, the photographer focuses on one location and then moves the camera with the action. When the person or object reaches the prefocused spot, the photographer clicks the shutter. The result is an image with a sharply focused point of interest and a blurry background. You can reproduce this effect in Adobe PhotoDeluxe by selecting what you want to keep sharp and then blurring the rest of the photo.

In this example the background was selected and then two special effects were applied—Blur and Wind. This combination of effects produced the image of a speeding red bullet.

Blur and Wind belong to a category of software known as **filters.** Filters apply mathematical calculations to the pixels in a photo to produce the special effects, such as blurring, softening, swirling, pinching, and so on. Adobe PhotoDeluxe has many built-in filters. You can also buy filters from other companies as plug-ins, which you can add to the Adobe PhotoDeluxe program.

Adding motion to a photo 127

1 Open the photo and select what to want to blur

Click Get Photo>Open Photo to open the photo.

To make the selection, click Modify and then choose a selection tool from the pop-up menu in the Select menu.

In this example the background needed to be blurred to give the impression that the car is streaming by the houses. The car is an almost solid color, so it was easier to select the car using several clicks of the Color Wand rather than using the selection tools to trace around the edges of the car.

The wheels were not included in the selection so that they would be part of the blurred area, reinforcing the illusion of movement. The selection was then inverted to select the background.

2 Blur the selection

Blurring is what gives the impression of movement. By not blurring some areas, you can create the impression that they are moving while the background remains still.

Click Modify>Effects>Special Effects>Blur>Soften.

Drag the slider to indicate how much blurring.

Click OK to apply the blur.

You can preview the effect for some Adobe PhotoDeluxe filters in either the dialog box or in the photo itself. See "Changing brightness and contrast" on page 87 for information on using the preview in the dialog box.

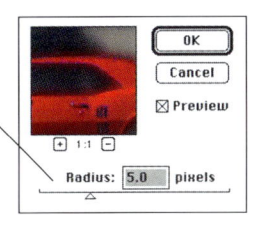

3 Apply the Wind effect

The Wind filter adds the final touch to the motion. The streaking produced by this filter makes the car really move. You can choose from three Wind effects and two directions. Preview each of them until you get an effect you like.

Select the wind type.

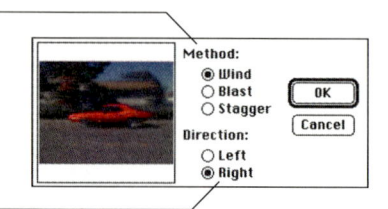

Select the direction.

Click OK to apply the wind.

Wind option   Blast option   Stagger option

When you've finished applying special effects, click Done to return to the other Modify buttons.

4 Save the photo

Click Save/Print>Save>Save.

You're ready to print the photo, save it as an Acrobat file, save it in a slide show, or export it into another format to send it via e-mail or display it on the Internet or your personal Web page.

5 Variations

When the background is dark or monochromatic, apply the motion filter to the main part of the photo. The effect is as if the camera was moving and the objects were still but you still get the idea of movement.

For a more sophisticated motion blur effect, choose File>Long Menus and then choose Effects>Blur>Motion Blur. This filter lets you set an angle and distance for the blurring. The angle determine where the movement is coming from and the distance determines how long the streaks are.

Drawing a pattern

Although Adobe PhotoDeluxe is not a drawing program, its selection and painting tools can help you with some drafting tasks, such as designing a pattern, drawing a floor plan, or creating a simple chart.

Adobe PhotoDeluxe works best when you're drawing rectangles, squares, or other geometric shapes. This doesn't mean the pattern can't be complex—putting one shape inside another or placing a shape on top of a texture can produce some very intricate patterns.

Patterns are not only fun, they're also useful when you're trying to visualize a larger design. For example, you can duplicate a simple element. You can use a pattern to fill another shape or to add interest to the dull part of a photo. Want a new shirt or dress? Just create the pattern and dress yourself digitally. Want to see what a different floor might do for your kitchen, new tiles for your bathroom, or new wallpaper for your bedroom? Take a photo of the old, funky room and then cover the walls or floor with your own custom patterns.

In this technique the pattern is meant to be used as a block in a quilt design. This pattern is made up of five squares. The simple shape and clear, clean colors produce a pleasing pattern that is easy to duplicate. To see how this pattern looks when it's repeated, see "Working with a grid" on page 163.

Drawing a pattern 131

1 ### Create a new file and turn on long menus

In this technique you create a new Adobe PhotoDeluxe file to serve as your "drafting board." To create a new file, choose File>New. Name the file and enter dimensions to fit your pattern size. Set the resolution to 72 if you plan to display the pattern on the screen or to 150 if you're going to print the pattern.

Just as you need tools to do mechanical drawing, you need digital tools to draw in Adobe PhotoDeluxe. The most essential of these are rulers. To turn on the rulers, you must be working in long menus. To turn on long menus, choose File>Long Menus. For more information about long menus, see "Using menus" on page 27.

To display the rulers, choose View>Show Rulers. Rulers are particularly helpful when you're drawing geometric shapes or placing objects on a grid. In this example the rulers are used to measure the squares for the quilt design. To turn off the rulers, choose View>Hide Rulers.

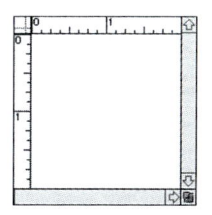

When you're drawing a pattern, you may need to have a bigger space to draw in. To get more area but still keep the same dimensions, magnify the window by choosing View>Zoom Out and then resize the window.

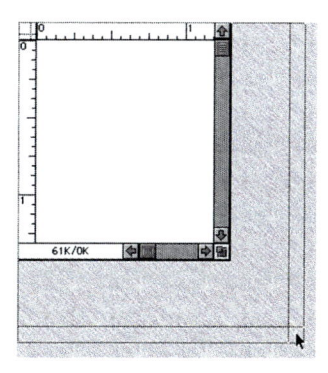

2 ### Draw and fill the first element of the pattern

In this example the pattern is built around a square, so the Square selection tool was used to draw the pattern. You can choose selection tools from the Select menu instead of using the Select palette. Choose Select>Selection Tools and then choose a tool from the submenu.

Special Effects

To draw the square, the cursor was placed at the upper left corner of the window and dragged to the 1-inch ruler marks along the top and left edges of the window.

To fill an area with a solid color, you can use the Selection Fill button. If you don't want to set an opacity or blend, however, the Color Change tool provides a quicker alternative.

Click Modify>Tools>Color Change, or choose Tools> Color Change.

Click the color box to select a color from the Color Swatches palette, then click inside the selection to fill it.

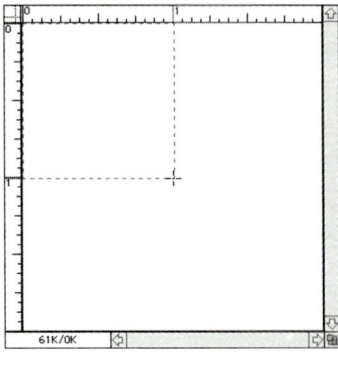

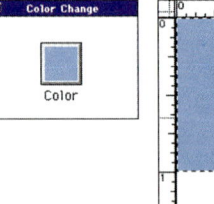

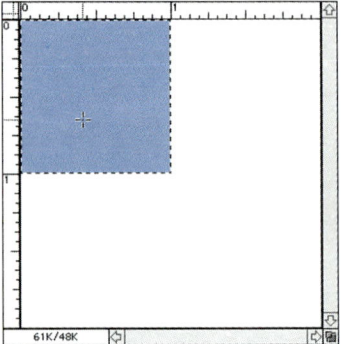

3 Duplicate, move, and fill other elements

To create the pattern, copy and paste the elements. You can click the Copy and Paste buttons, choose Edit>Copy and Edit>Paste, or press the Command-C and Command-V keyboard shortcuts.

If you copy and paste without deselecting, the copied selection appears over the current selection. If you deselect, the selection appears in the center of the window. When you're using long menus, you can press Command-D to deselect.

> The fastest way duplicate a selection is to hold down the Option key as you drag the selection.

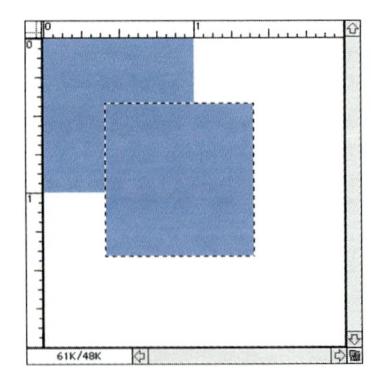

To fill the elements, use the Color Change button or choose Tools>Color Change. You can also use the Selection Fill or Gradient Fill button, or choose these commands from the Effects menu.

As a final touch, a border was added around this pattern. To create the border, Command-D was used to deselect the last element, then Command-A was used to select the entire window. (The Command-D and Command-A keyboard shortcuts are only available when you're working in long menus.)

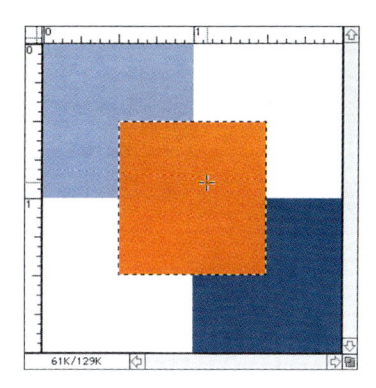

To add a border, click Modify>Effects>Outline, or choose Effects>Outline.

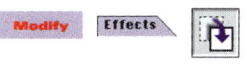

Enter a value for the border width.

Click to indicate where to start the border.

Click to select a border color.

Set an opacity or blend (optional).

Click OK to create the border.

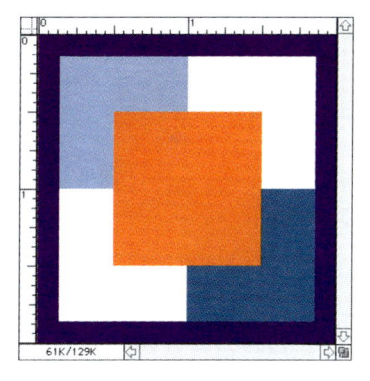

4 Save the photo

Click Save/Print>Save>Save.

You're ready to print the photo, save it as an Acrobat file, save it in a slide show, or export it into another format to send it via e-mail or display it on the Internet or your personal Web page.

Special Effects

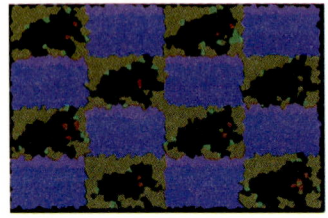

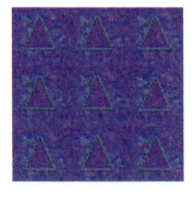

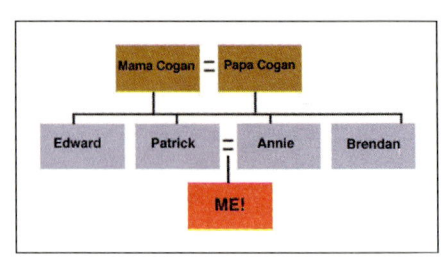

5 Variations

Apply filters to patterns for interesting effects

Create simple charts

To create a fast and dirty pattern element, use a selection tool to draw a shape, fill it with color, and then use one of the filters to add texture.

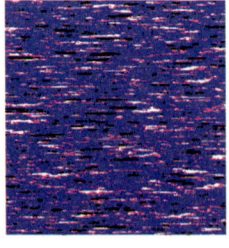

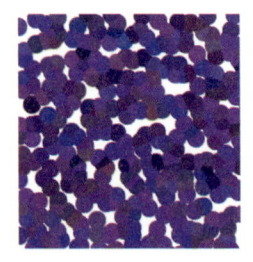

Solid fill   Mezzotint filter   Pointillize filter   Noise filter

You can also use the Color Change button to fill adjacent areas that are the same color, without making a selection. Just as the Color Wand selects areas that are similar in color, Color Change fills areas that are similar in color. The background in this example was filled using Color Change.

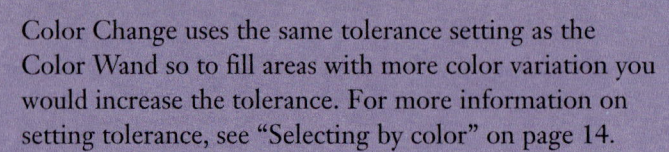

Color Change uses the same tolerance setting as the Color Wand so to fill areas with more color variation you would increase the tolerance. For more information on setting tolerance, see "Selecting by color" on page 14.

Showing a photo through text

One of the hottest looks in print advertising today is the display of a photo or other graphic through text, sometimes called **masking** (because the type blocks out parts of the photo). You can reproduce this effect quickly and easily using Adobe PhotoDeluxe layers.

In this example the text was used to create a business logo. Whatever you're designing, your first goal is to get the attention of your audience. Keep in mind that a simple, straightforward design often has more impact than a multicolored graphic extravaganza. Use a design that moves the eye in a specific direction and toward the key information—for example, from left to right, top to bottom, or on a strong diagonal.

The ability to paste photos inside text opens up a new world for your creative imagination. Use this technique to liven up business cards, product labels, report covers, slide show titles, PTA announcements, For Sale posters, party invitations—the list is endless.

Using a photo behind the text adds interest to a printed document without taking up any more space on the printed page. The logo in this example was designed so that it can be resized to fit on cards, letterhead, envelopes, or brochures. It establishes an instant and arresting business identity.

Special Effects

1 Copy the photo to the Clipboard

Because you want to have the photo available once you've created the text, open the photo, copy it to the Clipboard, and then close the photo. Don't save any changes.

Click Get Photo>Open Photo to open the photo and then click Modify>Edit>Copy to copy the photo to the Clipboard.

2 Create a new file

To create a new file, choose File>New. Name the file and enter the dimensions for your logo, card, flyer, or brochure. Set the resolution to 150 if you're going to print the card on your desktop printer. If you're having the card or flyer printed professionally, ask the printing center what resolution they require. For more information on setting resolutions, see "Getting photos into Adobe PhotoDeluxe" on page 5.

When you have a photo stored on the Clipboard, Adobe PhotoDeluxe automatically enters the dimensions and resolution of that file in the New dialog box, making the new file exactly the same size and resolution as the Clipboard contents. This ensures that the photo will fill any text you create in this file. If you want to have some room to maneuver the text after it's pasted, make the new file smaller than the photo dimensions.

3 Add and manipulate the text

Like all Adobe PhotoDeluxe files, the new file has one layer. If you don't have a checkerboard pattern on, the layer appears white, but it's actually transparent. If you print on colored paper, the text will appear to float on the colored background. If you want white to surround the text, fill this layer with white. See "Displaying transparent areas of a layer" on page 23 for more information on layer transparency.

Showing a photo through text 137

Click Modify>Tools>Text to display the Text dialog box.

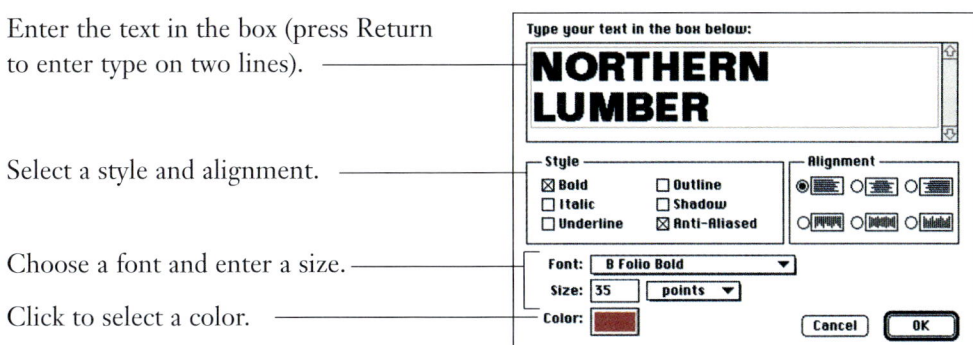

Enter the text in the box (press Return to enter type on two lines).

Select a style and alignment.

Choose a font and enter a size.

Click to select a color.

Click OK to add the text.

Drag to position the text.

If the text is too big or too small, or if you don't like the font, press the Delete key, then click the Text tool to try again.

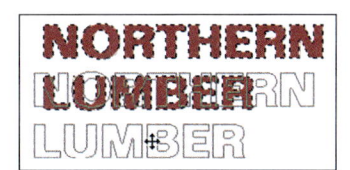

> Don't click the None button to get rid of the text. This deselects the text and makes it part of the layer. If you do this, you'll have to delete the layer to get rid of the text.

To add impact to the Northern Lumber logo, the text was distorted before the photo was pasted. You can apply many different kinds of resizing and distortion to the text in your design (or to any other selection). In this example the text was given an unusual perspective.

To distort a selection, click Modify>Size>Distort. Handles appear around the selection, which you drag to change the selection shape.

Drag the handles to distort. To apply the distortion, click inside the box with the OK cursor. To try again, click outside the box with the cancel cursor.

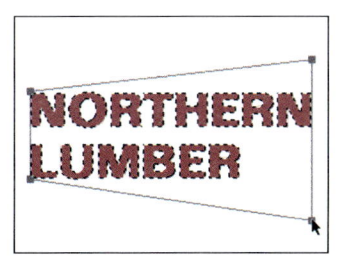

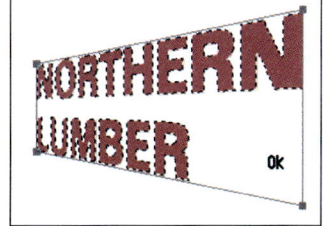

4 Paste the photo into the text

The photo must be pasted while the text is still selected. (If you've deselected the text, use the Color Wand to select the transparent areas on the text layer and then invert the selection.) The photo is pasted behind the selection. Although only part of the photo is showing, the entire photo is still available. This means you can move the photo around until the right part is visible.

Click Modify>Edit>Paste Into to paste the photo.

Drag the photo to change the part of the photo you're seeing. The selection border shows you the edges of the photo.

When the photo is in the right place, click None to deselect the text.

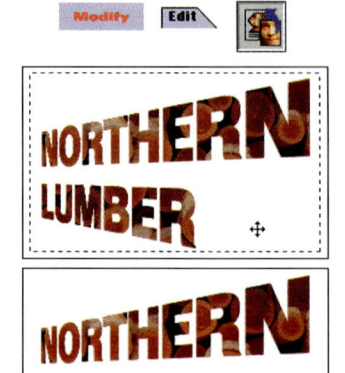

5 Save the photo

Click Save/Print>Save>Save.

You're ready to print the photo, save it as an Acrobat file, save it in a slide show, or export it into another format to send it via e-mail or display it on the Internet or your personal Web page.

Showing a photo through text   139

6 Variations

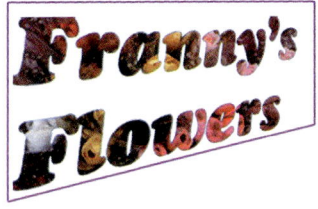

When you're displaying a photo through text, think about what part of the text you want to show and the relative sizes of the photo file and the font. If you're using a large point size for the text, be sure the photo is big enough to fill the letters without resizing. If you want a specific part of the photo to show through, make the text the right shape so that you can drag the part you want into the letters. It's easy to check the size of a photo. Every photo has a number in the lower left corner of the window. This number normally shows the file size. You can use this box to display the dimensions of the photo.

```
Width: 432 pixels (6 inches)
Height: 288 pixels (4 inches)
Channels:   3 (RGB Color)
Resolution: 72 pixels/inch
```

365K/365K

To check the photo dimensions, click in the size box and hold down the mouse button.

Creating backgrounds with filters

You don't always have to substitute one background for another to make a dramatic change in a photo. Using one of Adobe PhotoDeluxe's special effects, or filters, you can transform an ordinary background into a mind-boggling setting. Using two or more filters moves you into a whole new dimension.

Selecting a background can sometimes be tricky. When you're filtering a background, however, you can be a little less precise in your selection. You'll be distorting the photo anyway, so in most cases the selection edges are not distinguishable in the final image.

Every filter effect dialog box offers a wide variety of options. Don't be shy—go ahead and try them all. It's wise, however, to demonstrate some restraint within a single image. Too many special effects, like too many typefaces, can obfuscate rather than enhance.

In this technique the Blur filter was used to create the "outer space" burst in the background. (It could be that the rocket ship just took off, leaving this trio behind for the humans to deal with!)

Creating backgrounds with filters 141

1 Open the photo and select the background

In this example there was no easy way to isolate the boys from the background. A combinations of selection tools was used to make the selection.

Click Get Photo>Open Photo to open the photo.

Click Modify and then choose a selection tool from the pop-up menu in the Select palette.

In this photo the Rectangle tool was used to select large areas and then the Trace tool was used to complete the outline around the bodies.

When you're using the Trace tool, trace small areas at a time. That way, if you make a mistake you can undo just the last addition. For more information see "Making selections" on page 13.

2 Apply the special effects

To select an Adobe PhotoDeluxe filter, click Modify>Effects>Special Effects and then click a category: Artistic, Fun, Blur, or Cool. Click a button in the category to apply a filter.

When you're finished applying the filters, click the Done tab to return to the other Modify buttons.

Special Effects

The Blur>Circular filter was used to create the spacy background in this example.

Select a method.

Enter an amount.

Select a quality.

Click OK to blur.

Click the Undo button to try out other effects. If you want to keep several filter effects while you're deciding which one to use, copy the selection to the Clipboard, create a new layer, paste the selection on the layer, and then apply the filters to the separate layers. Turn the layers on and off to see the different effects. For more information see "Using layers to try out effects" on page 111.

3 Save the photo

Click Save/Print>Save>Save.

You're ready to print the photo, save it as an Acrobat file, save it in a slide show, or export it into another format to send it via e-mail or display it on the Internet or your personal Web page.

4 Variations

Wind filter

Pointillize filter

Find Edges filter (applied twice)

Circular Blur filter

Before you use special effects, make sure you have as much free memory as possible. It also helps to use the smallest possible files. If you still don't have enough memory, use the Rectangle tool to divide the photo into quadrants and filter each selection individually.

You can use the options in the Circular dialog box to vary your blur effects.

- The Zoom option blurs along radial lines, as if you were zooming in or out of the image.
- The Spin option blurs along concentric circular lines, as if you were spinning a wheel.
- The Quality options produce minor differences in the look of the blur. Draft quality is the fastest, but produces grainy results. The Good and Best settings produce smoother results and are virtually indistinguishable except on large selections.
- To specify the origin of a circular blur, drag the lines in the Blur center box, as shown in the following examples.

Origin in center

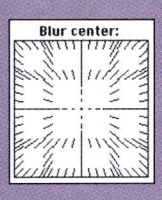

Origin in upper left corner

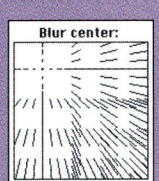

Combining different types of photos

Every time you combine two or more photos in an Adobe PhotoDeluxe image, you're creating a photo collage. Although the final image is usually very rewarding, building a collage in a darkroom involves sandwiching negatives, trial-and-error exposure, and lots of patience. Using Adobe PhotoDeluxe layers, however, collage creation becomes an hour of pleasurable entertainment.

A collage is built in stages. Before you begin, spend some time planning. Try to find photos in which people are the same size and are standing or sitting in similar or compatible positions. You can resize the photos if necessary, but you don't want the changes to be so dramatic that you introduce noticeable distortion. Decide which photo will provide the background, and get a general idea of where the other photos will go. When you select the pieces for the collage, be sure to leave yourself some creative freedom. As you rearrange and mix photos, you'll come up with ideas that never even occurred to you.

A collage can be made up of more than family photographs—you can add clip art or use stock photos to provide glamorous backgrounds. And you don't need to stop with the photo. Try gluing pieces of cloth, newspaper, or other textures to your final prints. This example combines new and old, color and black-and-white photos.

1 Open, select, and save the pieces of the collage

To prepare for the assembly stage, decide which photo will be your background photo and which photos you'll use pieces of. Open each photo you're going to paste in, select the area you want to use, and save the selections in the Hold Photo folder. In this example the photo of Grandpa was chosen as the background because he is sitting. It's easier to add people standing behind a chair than it would be to incorporate a chair into another photo. Besides, Grandpa offers the most interesting atmosphere.

Click Get Photo>Open Photo to open the photo.

Click Modify and then choose a selection tool from the pop-up menu in the Select palette. When you're selecting pieces for the collage, keep in mind that not all of each piece will be visible in the final image. Don't worry about selecting areas that won't show. For example, if a person will only be visible from the waist up, don't waste time selecting the legs and feet. You can also save time by trimming away parts of the photo that you don't need before making the selection.

The outdoorsman in this collage was selected by first trimming away most of the photo (Modify>Size>Trim). The Color Wand tool was used to select the background and then the Trace tool was used to complete the background selection. The selection was then deleted, leaving just the body on a transparent background.

Click Save/Print>Save>Hold Photo to save the edited selection in the Hold Photo folder.

Repeat this process for each photo piece you're going to add. If your final image will be black and white (or a sepia tone, like this example), you can convert color photos to black and white before you save them.

To convert a color photo, open it and click Modify>Effects>Color to BW.

In this example the second piece of the collage was converted to black and white. The background was selected using the Polygon and Trace tools and then deleted. Finally, the selection was saved in the Hold Photo folder.

2 Open the background photo and separate it into layers

In this example the two men need to end up behind Grandpa but in front of the arbor backdrop, so the photo must be split up into two selections and put on separate layers.

Click Modify and select the parts of the photo you want to be movable. In this example Grandpa was selected using the Rectangle and Trace tools. The area to the left of Grandpa was included in the selection to provide a good cover for the bottom part of the standing men.

The selection was copied to the Clipboard. The New button was used to create a new layer and the selection was pasted on the new layer. The selection was then deselected.

Although the photo still looks the same, you can check that the selection was placed on a separate layer by clicking the eye icon beside the bottom layer. (The selection is still on the bottom layer too, but that doesn't matter because it will be covered up by the copy on this layer.)

Combining different types of photos 147

3 Add the other photos

You're ready to assemble your collage.

Click the Hold Photo bar to display the contents of the Hold Photo folder. Drag the photo, select the photo and click Paste Layer, or double-click the photo to add it to the open window.

When you release the mouse button, the Make Layer dialog box appears. Name the layer and click OK. The new layer appears on the top of the Layers palette.

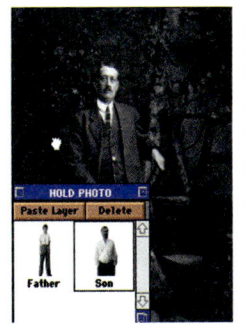

To place the grandson behind Grandpa, his layer was dragged down in the layers palette so that it was below Grandpa but above the background.

As a final step the grandson was resized and then dragged into position. To resize a layer, click Modify>Size>Resize.

Drag a handle to resize. When you have the size you want, click inside the box with the OK cursor. To cancel the resizing and try again, click outside the box with the cancel cursor.

Follow these four steps for each additional piece: drag the photo from the Hold Photo folder, rearrange the layer, resize the selection, and drag into position.

The order of the steps can vary; in this example the last piece was first moved into position and then resized.

4 Save the photo

Click Save/Print>Save>Save.

You're ready to print the photo, save it as an Acrobat file, save it in a slide show, or export it into another format to send it via e-mail or display it on the Internet or your personal Web page.

5 Variations

Combine color and black and white just for the cool effect

Tint the photo (see "Tinting a black-and-white photo" on page 72.)

Create impossible time warps

Using text as a background

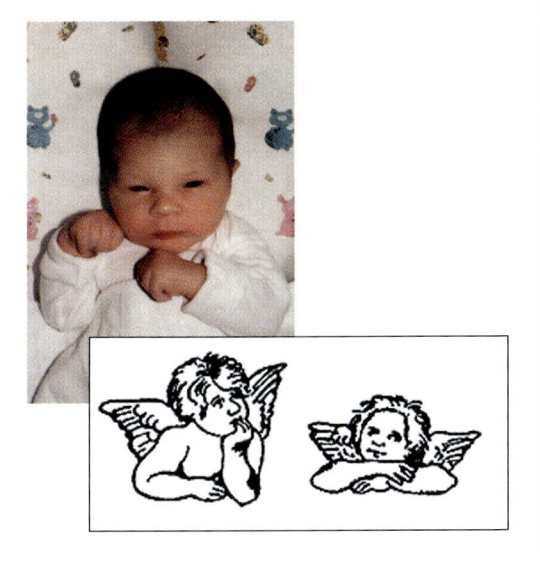

The text in an image is usually the main conveyer of information. It names the company, tells the time and place, or entertains the audience. You can also use text as an effective background. To make the text less obvious, choose a simple font and small size. Repeating a few words or phrases transforms the text into a pattern and focuses attention on the photo.

Clip art is a quick and easy way to add interest to a photo. Most clip art consists of black-and-white line drawings or sketches, but you can also get collections of three-dimensional, color clip art. When you buy clip art, you also buy the right to use the art in your own work. Ask your computer dealer for some clip-art catalogs and spend a few happy hours browsing. You'll be amazed at all the cool things you can add to your pictures!

In this example the baby photo is on one layer, the text is on another layer, and the clip art is on a third. Color was used to fill the text layer, the text itself, and the clip art. To achieve some unusual effects, try leaving white in the image, use a gradient fill for the background or text, or position the photo off-center in the image.

Special Effects

1. Open, select, and save the clip art or other photos you'll use

If you're simply putting text behind a photo, you don't need to do this step. In this example only one piece of clip art was added to the final image, so it was copied to the Clipboard. If you're using multiple photos or graphics, open them, select the pieces you want to use, and save the pieces in the Hold Photo folder.

2. Open the main photo and and make any editing changes

Click Get Photo>Open Photo to open the photo.

If you're using only part of the photo, click Modify and choose a selection tool from the pop-up menu in the Select palette. In this example the entire photo was used.

Your photo may already have the space you need to add the text. In this example, canvas was added to make room for the text around the photo. Some color was also added to provide contrast for the text.

To add canvas to a photo, click Modify>Size>Canvas Size.

Enter new dimensions. (In this example 2 inches was added to the width and the height.)

Click to indicate where you want the photo in relation to the canvas. (Clicking the center box adds the canvas equally around the edges of the photo.)

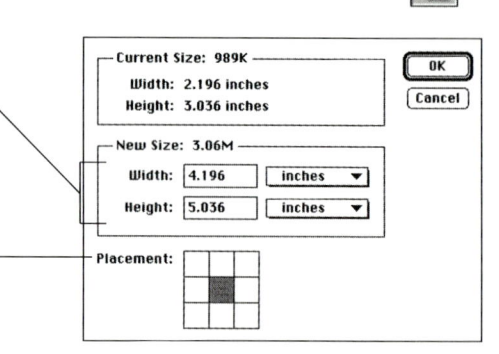

Current Size: 989K
Width: 2.196 inches
Height: 3.036 inches

New Size: 3.06M
Width: 4.196 inches
Height: 5.036 inches

Placement:

Click OK to increase the canvas size.

Added canvas is transparent. If you want a color backdrop for the text, you can fill a layer with color and then place this layer under the photo.

Click New to create a layer. Name the layer and click OK. In the Layers palette, drag the layer down to the bottom so that it's behind the photo.

Using text as a background

To fill the layer, use the Color Change button. Color Change fills all adjacent areas that are the same color. This layer is transparent, so one click fills the entire layer with color.

Click Modify>Tools>Color Change.

Select a color from the Color Swatches palette and click in the layer to fill. Make sure the layer you want to fill is the active layer; otherwise you'll cover up the photo.

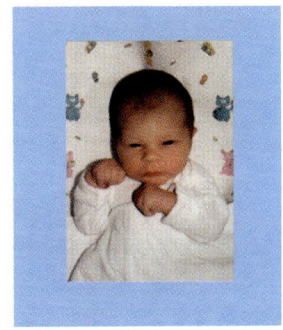

3 Add the text

Now you're ready to add the text. After you decide what text you're going to add, you'll need to try out different sizes and placements to get the effect you want.

Click Modify>Tools>Text to create the text.

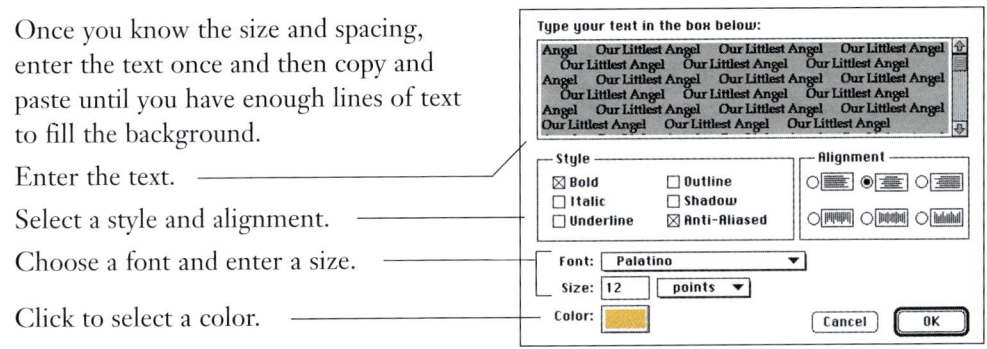

Once you know the size and spacing, enter the text once and then copy and paste until you have enough lines of text to fill the background.

Enter the text.

Select a style and alignment.

Choose a font and enter a size.

Click to select a color.

Click OK to add the text.

Depending on what layer was active, you may need to drag the Text layer so that it is above the Fill layer and below the Photo layer.

> New layers always appear above the active layer.

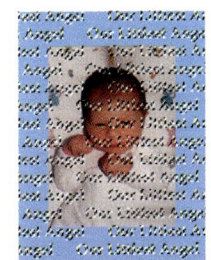

4 Add and color the clip art

Add the clip art or any additional photos you're using. If you're dragging a photo from the Hold Photo folder, a new layer is made automatically. In this example the art was stored on the Clipboard, so a new layer had to be created before the art was pasted.

Click the New button to create a layer. Name the layer and click OK. If necessary, drag the art layer in the Layers palette until it's on top of all the other layers.

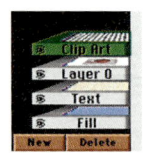

Clip art often comes on a white background. If the art is on an opaque background, use the Color Wand tool to select the background. You want to be left with the art selected, so invert the selection and click Modify>Edit>Delete Background. This leaves the art selected on a transparent background.

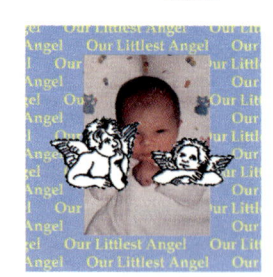

To add color to the art, click Modify>Effects>Selection Fill.

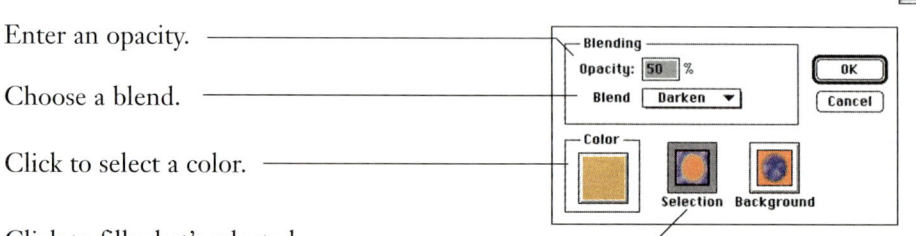

Enter an opacity.

Choose a blend.

Click to select a color.

Click to fill what's selected.

Click OK to fill the selection.

In this example the art was filled with a 50% opacity and the Darken blend was used.

As a final step the art was deselected. Each angel was individually selected with the Rectangle tool and dragged into position.

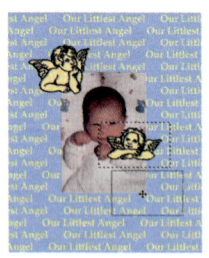

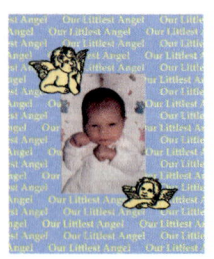

Using text as a background   **153**

5 Save the photo

Click Save/Print>Save>Save.

You're ready to print the photo, save it as an Acrobat file, save it in a slide show, or export it into another format to send it via e-mail or display it on the Internet or your personal Web page.

6 Variations

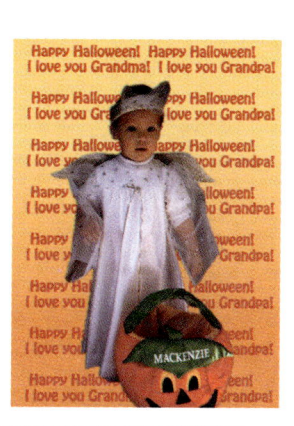

The placement box in the Canvas Size dialog box indicates where the new canvas will be added in relation to the original photo. You can place the photo in one of nine positions. Here are a few examples of using different placements.

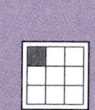

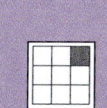

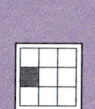

Photo in upper left corner   Photo in upper right corner   Photo in middle left

One of the easiest way to add color to line art is to fill the selection using the Darken blend. When you choose Darken, the black from the original art shows through the fill color.

Filled with Normal blend   Filled with Darken blend

Duplicating, flipping, and rotating selections

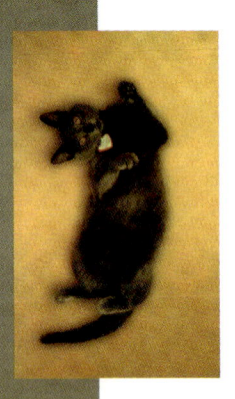

All you pet owners knows that your dog, cat, pig, or parrot makes an irresistible photographic model. A simple photo of your animal can be a jumping-off point for a much more adventurous photo. Putting a selection on one layer and the background on another lets you duplicate, resize, flip, and rotate a selection as much as you want, without affecting the background.

Replacing a background is an easy way to save photos that have wonderful expressions but are diminished by distracting or dull backgrounds. Substituting one photo for another is one way to add interest. When you want to focus attention on a charming subject, however, filling with a color provides less competition for the main attraction.

In this technique a gradient fill was substituted for the original background and then modified using the Twirl filter. The cat was duplicated, resized, rotated, and flipped and then laid over the new background.

Duplicating, flipping, and rotating selections

1. Open a photo and select the area you want to manipulate

Click Get Photo>Open Photo to open the photo.

Click Modify and choose a selection tool from the pop-up menu in the Select palette.

In this example the solid yellow background was selected using the Color Wand tool. The background was then deleted, leaving the cat on a transparent background.

The background appears white, even though it has been deleted. For information on changing how transparency is displayed, see "Displaying transparent areas of a layer" on page 23.

2. Store the selection in the Hold Photo folder

In this example the cat was saved in the Hold Photo folder. You could copy the cat to the Clipboard, but because you want to place it on a separate layer you would then have to create a layer before pasting the selection.

Click Save/Print>Save>Hold Photo.

3. Create the new background

If you're using another photo as the new background, open the photo. In this example a new background file was created, filled with a gradient, and then filtered to produce the "lost in space" look.

If you're creating a new file, choose File>New.

Enter a name.

Enter dimensions.

Enter a resolution to fit your printer.
Click OK to create the file.

For more information on setting image resolution, see "Getting photos into Adobe PhotoDeluxe" on page 5.

Special Effects

To add a gradient, click All in the Select palette to select the entire image and then click Modify>Effects> Gradient Fill.

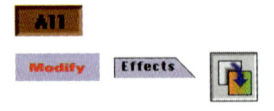

Click to select a start color.

Click to select an end color.

Click to fill what's selected.

Click a direction. (In this example the gradient moves from left to right.)

Click OK to fill.

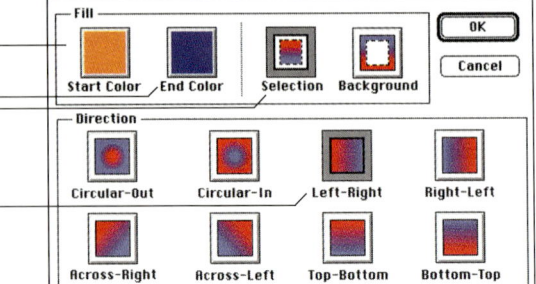

Adding some stark, bold color to the gradient makes the filter more effective. In this example the Brush tool was used to paint some brush strokes in the background.

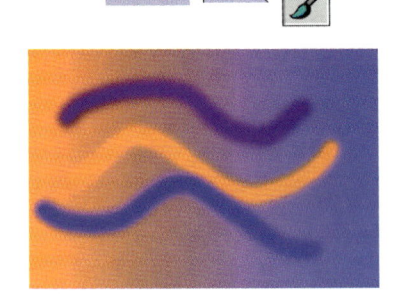

As a final touch, the Twirl filter was applied.

Drag the slider to set the distortion.

Click OK to apply the twirl.

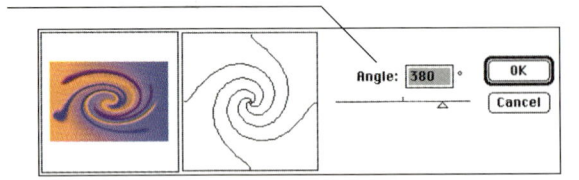

Click the Done tab to leave the Special Effects area.

Duplicating, flipping, and rotating selections 157

4 Paste the selection and manipulate

As long as the selection is on its own layer, you can do anything you like to it without affecting the background. You might want to create several layers and paste the selection on each one so you can try out different effects on different layers.

Click the Hold Photo bar to display the contents of the Hold Photo folder. Drag the photo, select the photo and click Paste Layer, or double-click the photo to add it to the open window.

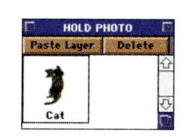

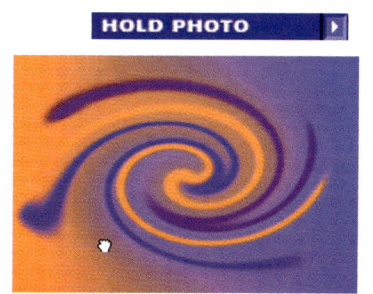

When you release the mouse button, the Make Layer dialog box appears. Name the layer and click OK. The new layer appears on the top of the Layers palette. The photo appears in the middle of the window.

With the photo on its layer, you're ready to roll. In this example the cat was resized, duplicated, and rotated. Before the cat could be manipulated, it had to be selected.

Even though the cat is displayed again a gradient, it still has a transparent background in its own layer. To select an object on a transparent background, click the Color Wand in a transparent area, and then click Invert to select the object. Copy this selection to the Clipboard so you can paste copies on this or other layers.

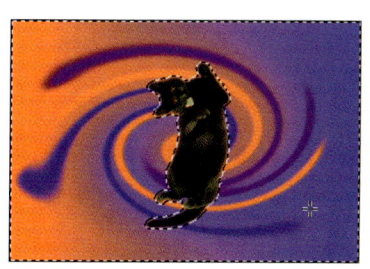

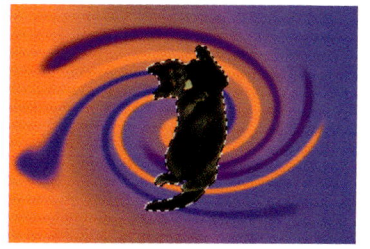

158   **Special Effects**

To resize a selection, click Modify>Size>Resize.

To resize, drag a handle and then click inside the box with the OK cursor. To cancel and try again, click outside the box with the cancel cursor.

To duplicate a selection, press Option and drag.

To rotate and flip a selection, click Modify> Orientation and then click a direction button— Rotate Left, Rotate Right, Free Rotate, Flip Horizontal, or Flip Vertical.

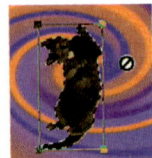

5 Save the photo

Click Save/Print>Save>Save.

You're ready to print the photo, save it as an Acrobat file, save it in a slide show, or export it into another format to send it via e-mail or display it on the Internet or your personal Web page.

6 Variations

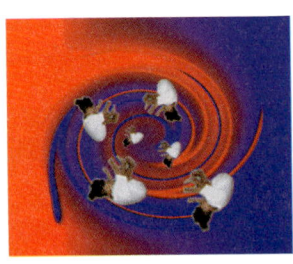

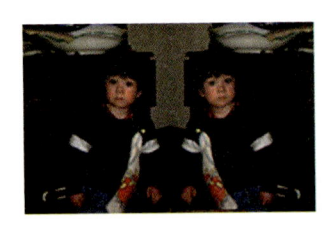

Creating a kaleidoscope effect

Although there are millions of effects you can produce using Adobe PhotoDeluxe, the day may come when you want MORE! When you hit that point, or when you see an incredibly cool effect in a book or magazine, you're ready to investigate the world of **plug-ins**—extensions to Adobe PhotoDeluxe that make it even more powerful. Adobe PhotoDeluxe comes with several kinds of built-in plug-ins: filter plug-ins for creating special effects, device plug-ins for controlling a camera or scanner, and format plug-ins for exporting to other file formats.

There is also a huge variety of third-party plug-ins available for use with Adobe PhotoDeluxe (any plug-in that works with Adobe Photoshop 3.0 or later will work with Adobe PhotoDeluxe). Samples of third-party plug-ins from a company called Metatools are included in the Cool section of Special Effects. These plug-ins are from an application called Kai's Power Tools (KPT). When you're ready to expand your repertoire, check your computer dealer and mail-order catalogs for other plug-in sources.

This example uses the KPT Vortex plug-in on a drawing. The Vortex filter divides the image into pieces called **tiles** and then scrambles them to produce a kaleidoscope effect. You can use this filter on a pattern, a photo, a selection, or a single layer. The effects are so varied and interesting that you could easily spend hours experimenting with this plug-in alone.

Special Effects

1 Open a photo or create a new file

Filters usually work best on drawings or photos that contain a variety of colors. You can use bold or muted colors for a more subtle effect. In this example the filter was applied to a simple drawing over a background gradient.

If you're applying the filter to a photo, click Get Photo>Open Photo.

If you're creating a new file, choose File>New.

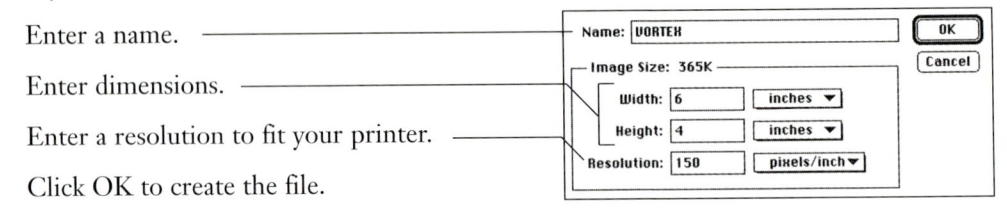

Enter a name.

Enter dimensions.

Enter a resolution to fit your printer.

Click OK to create the file.

For more information on setting image resolution, see "Getting photos into Adobe PhotoDeluxe" on page 5.

To add a gradient, click All in the Select palette to select the entire image and then click Modify>Effects>Gradient Fill.

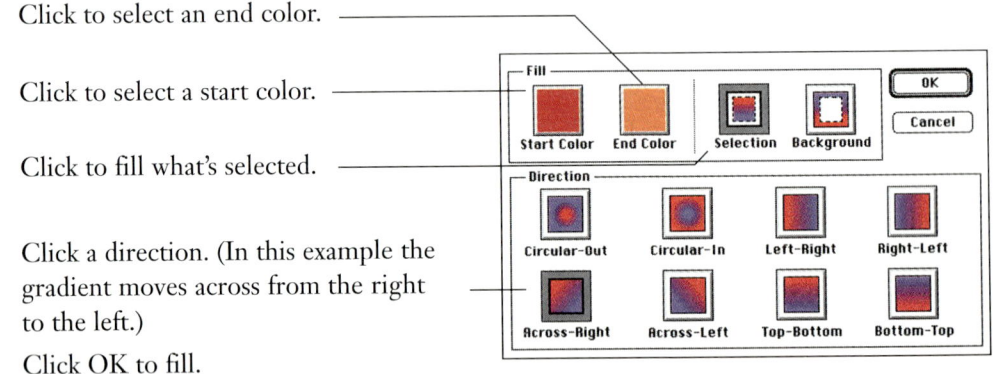

Click to select an end color.

Click to select a start color.

Click to fill what's selected.

Click a direction. (In this example the gradient moves across from the right to the left.)

Click OK to fill.

When you're happy with the result, click None in the Select palette to deselect the entire image.

Creating a kaleidoscope effect 161

Adding some color or shape inside the fill gives the filter even more to play with. You can draw using any selection tool except the Color Wand.

In this example the Rectangle tool was used to draw a shape, which was then outlined with a color border.

To add a border, click Modify>Effects>Outline.

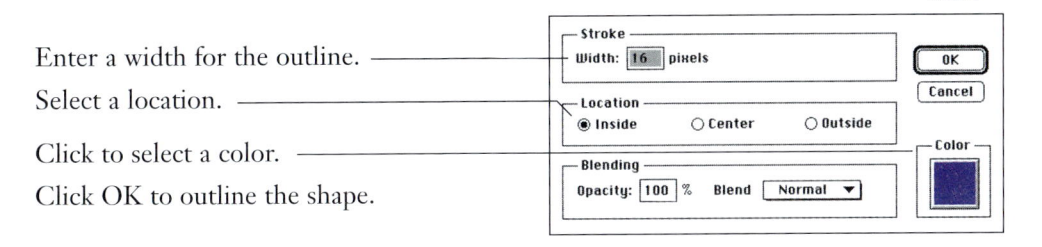

Enter a width for the outline.

Select a location.

Click to select a color.

Click OK to outline the shape.

Click None in the Select palette to deselect the rectangle. If you don't deselect, the filter is applied only to selected area.

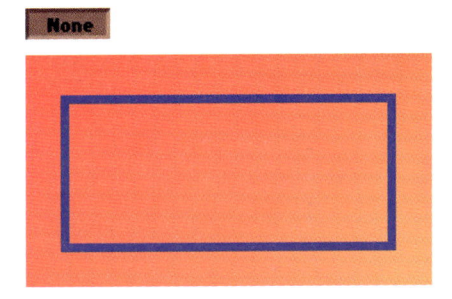

2 Apply the Vortex filter

Let the games begin!

To apply the filter, click Modify>Effects> Special Effects>Cool>KPT Vortex.

Special Effects

3 Save the photo

Click Save/Print>Save>Save.

You're ready to print the photo, save it as an Acrobat file, save it in a slide show, or export it into another format to send it via e-mail or display it on the Internet or your personal Web page.

4 Variations

Try other gradient directions

Turn photos into magic shapes

The Vortex filter divides the images into pieces, or tiles, and then applies the effect. You can change the size of the tiles by holding down a number key from 1 to 0 as you click the Vortex button. Press 1 as you click to use the largest tiles; press 0 to use the smallest tiles. The default setting is 5.

Original   Vortex (1)   Vortex (3)   Vortex (5)   Vortex (7)   Vortex (0)

Working with a grid

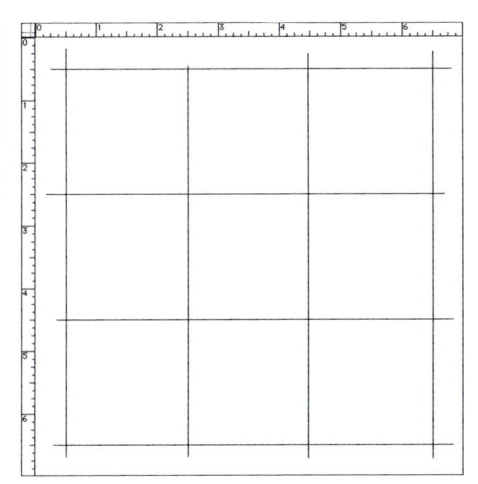

Any time you want to repeat and space an object in an image, it's a good idea to create a placement grid. You can draw the grid using one of the Adobe PhotoDeluxe tools, or you can scan a grid and then open it in Adobe PhotoDeluxe. By putting the grid on a separate layer, you can line up your shapes or objects precisely and then delete the layer when you're finished.

The grid doesn't need to be square, although this is the most common type of grid and the easiest to make. It could be circular, oval, or even a perspective guide. The idea is that you place the grid on a layer under the selection you're duplicating, and then eliminate the grid when you're finished. A grid is handy when you're placing multiple objects in an image, but it isn't limited to simple duplication. It's similar to using alignment when you've entered several lines of text.

In this technique the pattern created in "Drawing a pattern" on page 130 was duplicated and placed on a rectangular grid. This pattern was originally designed as a quilt block, so repeating the blocks on a larger rectangle realistically demonstrates how the finished quilt will look.

Special Effects

1 Open the pattern or object and save it in the Hold Photo folder

Because you want to have the pattern or object on a separate layer, it's easiest to copy it into the Hold Photo folder. That way, when you add it to the final image, it automatically goes on its own layer.

Click Get Photo>Open Photo to open the photo you want to use.

If you're selecting part of a photo, click Modify and choose a selection tool from the pop-up menu on the Select palette. Delete the parts of the photo you don't want. You need to end up with a shape on a transparent background. Because the entire block was used in this design, no selection was necessary before saving the file.

Click Save/Print>Save>Hold Photo to save the selection in the Hold Photo folder.

Repeat this process for each element you want to include in the pattern.

2 Create a new file and draw the grid

Create a new file that's large enough to accommodate the duplicated objects. For a rectangular grid, make the file as wide as it is high.

Choose File>New.

Enter a name.

Enter dimensions.

Enter a resolution to fit your printer.

Click OK to create the file.

For more information on setting image resolution, see "Getting photos into Adobe PhotoDeluxe" on page 5.

> Its easier to draw a grid if you have rulers showing in the window. To turn on the rulers, choose File>Long Menus and then choose View>Show Rulers. To turn off the rulers, choose View>Hide Rulers.

Working with a grid 165

To create the grid you draw a series of lines. Before you draw, you need to know the size of the objects you'll be copying to the grid. Then you can create the grid so that each square will hold one object. In this example the pattern pieces are each 2 inches square, so the grid is drawn in 2-inch increments.

Click Modify>Tools>Line.

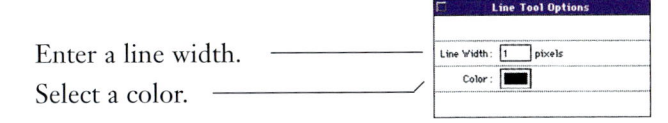

Enter a line width.

Select a color.

Draw vertical lines for the grid. (Lines were drawn at the 1/2", 2-1/2", 4-1/2" and 6-1/2" marks along the top ruler for this 2-inch grid.)

Draw horizontal lines for the grid. (Lines were drawn at the 1/2", 2-1/2", 4-1/2", and 6-1/2" marks along the side ruler for this 2-inch grid.)

After you've created the grid, save a copy of the file to use as a grid template with other photos.

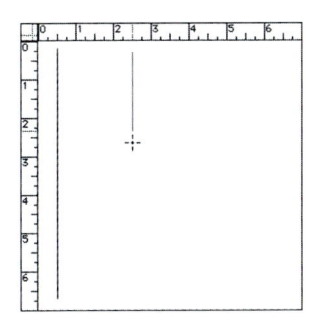

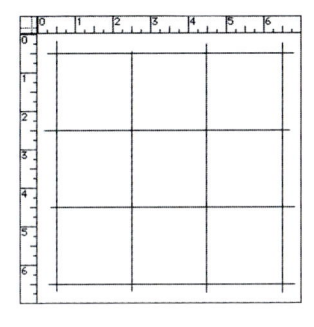

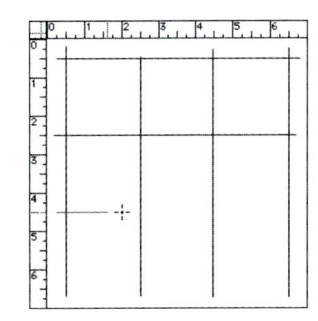

3 Add the objects and duplicate

Now you're ready to use the grid to place the pattern elements.

Click the Hold Photo bar to display the contents of the Hold Photo folder.

Drag the photo, select the photo and click Paste Layer, or double-click the photo to add it to the open window.

When you release the mouse button, the Make Layer dialog box appears. Name the layer and click OK. The new layer appears on the top of the Layers palette. The new image appears in the center of the window.

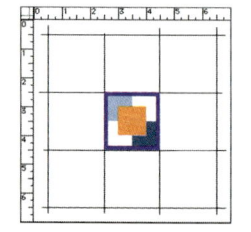

To fill the grid you need to select the object, duplicate it, and then drag the copies to new locations. You could copy, paste, and drag to duplicate and position the objects. It's much faster, however, to simply press Option as you drag the selection.

Click Modify and choose a selection tool from the pop-up menu in the Select palette. The Square tool was used to select this block.

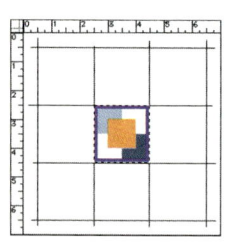

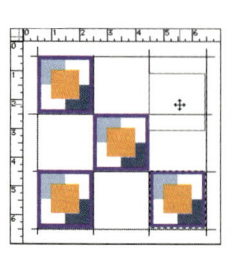

Press Shift plus Option as you drag to move the duplicate in a straight vertical or horizontal direction.

Use the arrow keys on your keyboard to nudge the selections in small increments.

Click None to deselect the last element.

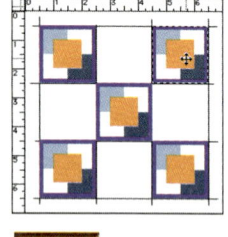

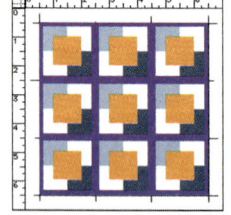

Working with a grid 167

4 Save the photo

Click the grid layer in the Layers palette to make it active and then click the Delete button in the Layers palette. In the dialog box, select the Delete Active Layer option and then click OK to delete the grid layer.

Click Save/Print>Save>Save.

You're ready to print the photo, save it as an Acrobat file, save it in a slide show, or export it into another format to send it via e-mail or display it on the Internet or your personal Web page.

5 Variations

Spread out the pattern and change colors

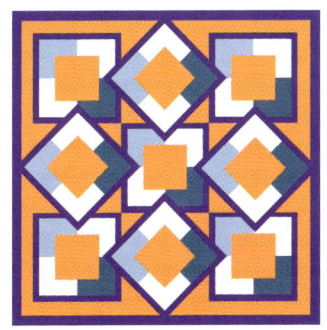

Rotate part of the pattern and fill the background

Use a symbol as a grid

To move a selection in larger increments, hold down Shift as you press the arrow keys.

If the edges between the objects don't line up exactly, you can draw a thin border around each piece. Select the object and then click Modify>Effects>Outline. In the Outline dialog box, click Outside to draw the border from the edge of the selection outward.

Replacing body parts

Here's the technique you've been waiting for! This one lets you keep all those great pictures of yourself—but get rid of former lovers, ex-spouses, obnoxious acquaintances, and old bosses. In addition to keeping current on your love life and fantasies, you can use this technique for visual matchmaking, replacing yourself with a better version from another photo, getting rid of closed eyes, flyaway or missing hair, or stupid smiles.

It's often easier to remove the offending person and fill in the background before you paste in the replacement. This helps eliminate size discrepancies and minimizes the seams that can appear where you overlay photos. In this example part of the background was used to fill the blank space left by the deleted head, but you can use any color or pattern that blends into the existing image. You then lay the replacement part over a more natural background.

The only down side to this technique is that you have to pick the parts you want to put together very carefully. Of course it's best if you can just paste the new piece over the old one, but the pieces are hardly ever exactly the right angle, color, position, or size. You need to be patient and have a good sense of humor when you're messing around with body parts.

168

1 Open, edit, and save the photo you're copying from

Before you begin realigning body parts, you may need to make edits to both photos. In this example the old boyfriend has to go—but be sure you have another one lined up before you sever the relationship.

Click Get Photo>Open Photo to open the photo.

When you're replacing body parts, nine times our of ten you will want to delete everything in the replacement picture except the part you're going to use. In most cases, this means deleting the background. Click Modify and choose a selection tool from the pop-up menu in the Select palette.

In this example the Color Wand tool was used to select the solid gray background, which was then deleted. The rest of the body was deleted when the head was pasted.

The background appears white even though it has been deleted. For information on changing how transparency is displayed, see "Displaying transparent areas of a layer" on page 23.

In this example the selection was saved in the Hold Photo folder. You could copy the selection to the Clipboard, but because you want to place it on a separate layer you would then have to create a layer before pasting the selection. When you use Hold Photo, Adobe PhotoDeluxe creates the new layer for you.

Click Save/Print>Save>Hold Photo.

2 Open and edit the photo you're modifying

With the replacement part safely in storage, you can start work on removing the one that's no longer needed. Rarely do the parts you're interchanging match up. One is bound to be a little bigger or smaller than the other, or at the wrong angle. To cover up these flaws, you replace the background and then graft the new part onto the body, instead of trying to do a simple cut and paste.

Special Effects

The first step is to select the background replacement. Click Modify and choose a selection tool from the pop-up menu in the Select palette that matches the shape you want to replace. In this example the Rectangle tool was used to select another part of the photo to cover up the space that would be deleted. Copy the selection to the Clipboard.

Next, select the area you want to replace. In this example the Rectangle tool was used and the selection was increased using the Trace tool.

To blend the new selection into the existing background, delete the current background using a feather edge. This softens the edges around the deleted area so the new selection fits in more smoothly.

Click Modify>Effects>Feather.

Enter a value to indicate how wide you want the soft edge to be.

Click to delete what's selected.

Click OK to feather and delete.

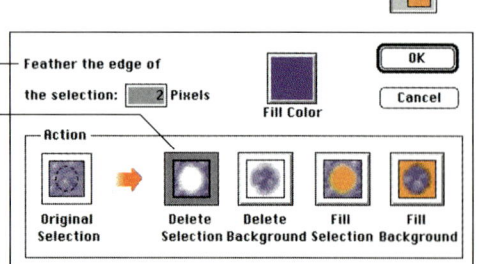

Click Modify>Edit>Paste Into.

Paste the rectangle from the Clipboard into the former head location.

Replacing body parts   171

Oops, too small! It's a shame there wasn't a larger area that could be copied, but there wasn't. If you need to enlarge the replacement, try resizing to stretch the selection. Because this is a feathered selection, there will be a little white left around the edges after resizing. If the selection hadn't been feathered, however, the resized rectangle would stand out from the background even more glaringly.

Click Modify>Size>Resize.

Drag one or more handles to resize the selection, then click inside the box with the OK cursor, or click outside the box with the cancel cursor to try again.

After resizing, click None in the Select palette to deselect.

3 Add and edit the replacement selection

Click the Hold Photo bar to display the contents of the Hold Photo folder. Drag the photo, select the photo and click Paste Layer, or double-click the photo to add it to the open window.

When you release the mouse button, the Make Layer dialog box appears. Name the layer and click OK. The new layer appears on the top of the Layers palette. The photo appears in the middle of the window.

You may have to do some clever editing to get the effects just right. In this example the new head needs to be moved, the suit needs to go, and the head is a wee bit small for the existing shoulders.

Special Effects

Drag if you need to move the selection.

Zoom in and use the Eraser tool to delete unwanted parts.

Zoom out and check the adjustments.

Use the Resize button to change the selection size.

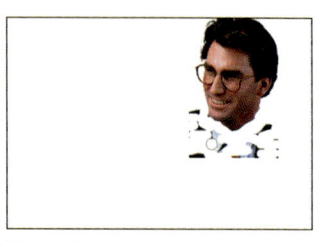

Turn off the background layer and use the Eraser tool to edit stray bits of leftovers.

View both layers to see the final image.

4 Save the photo

Click Save/Print>Save>Save.

You're ready to print the photo, save it as an Acrobat file, save it in a slide show, or export it into another format to send it via e-mail or display it on the Internet or your personal Web page.

5 Variations

Meet famous people

Move annoying objects.

Covering up problem areas

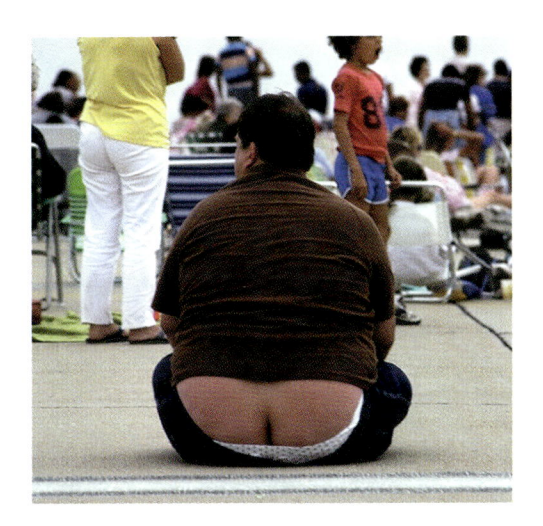

It seems that everyone has photographs with a "little problem." Maybe you were caught in almost-indecent exposure, or you didn't realize you had spilled red wine all over your white dress, or your brother-in-law was just trying to be funny. And of course there's the perennial problem of pure denial—can I really be that wide? In most cases, a little time with Adobe PhotoDeluxe can help redeem your self-esteem.

As long as a large enough section around the "embarrassment" is intact, you can select a color from the surrounding area and fill to eliminate the problem. Or you can copy and paste a selection over the offending part of the photo. Filling works best when you want to repair an area with a solid color. If you have enough "material" available, copy-and-paste works best to reconstruct prints, patterns, and textures.

As for the girth problem, some improvement is possible using the Pinch filter. However, pinching quickly produces noticeable distortion, so you have to use it in moderate doses. Your best bet is to go back on your diet and start getting up in the morning for your workout.

In this technique the pants were filled with a gradient that mimics the colors of the jeans. The edge of the selection was then smudged to disguise the border of the filled area. Finally, the body was selected and pinched slightly, so that a waist magically appeared.

Special Effects

1. Open the photo and select the offending area or a replacement area

Depending on the area you want to fix, you might need to select the area you want to get rid of and fill it, or you might be able to select an area near the problem and simply copy and paste a replacement.

Click Get Photo>Open File.

Click Modify and choose a selection tool from the pop-up menu in the Select palette.

If your photo has an area that's similar in shape, color, and texture to the part you want to cover up, select that area.

In this example the Color Wand was used the select the piece to be repaired.

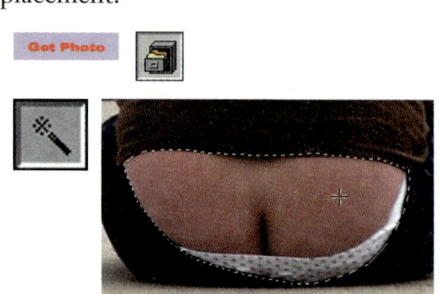

2. Repair the area

If you're using a replacement selection, press Option and drag the selection to duplicate it. Deselect once the selection is in place.

This photo doesn't have a piece of jeans that's big enough for cut and paste, so a fill was used to provide the missing fabric. Because there is some variation in the color of the jeans, a gradient fill proved to be a better approach than filling with a solid color.

Choose Modify>Effects>Gradient Fill.

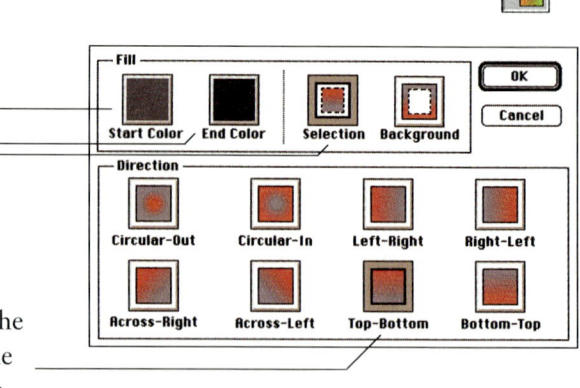

Click to select a start color.
Click to select an end color.
Click to fill what's selected.

Click a direction. (In this example the start color appears at the top and the end color appears the bottom of the selection.)

In most cases you select a start and end color for the gradient from the Color Swatches palette. When you're repairing an area, however, it's sometimes best to select colors from within the photo itself to get the closest match. For example, because of the color variation in these jeans, the start and end colors were selected from the photo. For more information about selecting colors from a photo, see "Selecting a color" on page 18.

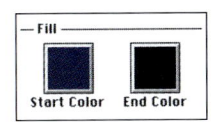

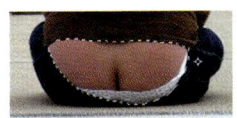

Selecting the start color

Selecting the end color

Once the colors are selected, click OK in the Gradient Fill dialog box to fill the selection. Then click None to deselect the selection.

In this example, after the selection was deselected, a small white edge was apparent around the selection border. The Smudge tool was used with a small, fine brush to blend the edges. When you want to make edges inconspicuous, it works best to smudge from the photo into the filled area. Use small strokes and check the effect after each stroke.

3 Make any other adjustments

At this point you might want to fix other areas or change the color of some parts of the photo, especially if the fill is too obvious. Maybe you want to use the Resize button to enlarge certain areas or the Trim button to cut out areas that you don't need.

In this example the body girth was reduced using the Pinch filter. The secret to using the Pinch filter is not to overdo it. Just as with any retouching, too much looks artificial. When you're using Pinch, too much introduces noticeable distortion. (Of course, that might be just the effect you're going for!)

Special Effects

Click Modify, choose a selection tool from the pop-up menu in the Select palette, and then select the area you want to pinch. The Color Wand and Trace tools were used to make this selection.

Click Modify>Effects>Special Effects>Fun>Pinch.

Drag the slider to indicate how much pinching you want. (The preview box shows the amount of distortion.)

Click OK to pinch.

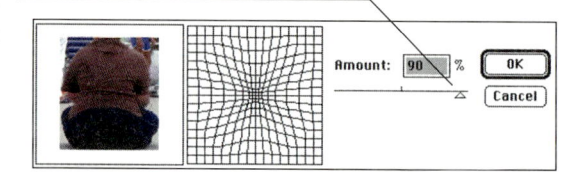

Before pinching

After pinching

After pinching, you might need to touch up areas that were inadvertently distorted when you applied the filter.

In this example some of the areas outside of the body were blurred during the pinch. The Brush tool with a hard-edged brush was used to repaint the areas. The paint color was selected from a surrounding area in the photo.

> Why not just use the Smudge tool to blend the edges? Because in this case the sharpness of the original needs to be brought back. Smudging would only increase the blurriness.

Covering up problem areas 177

4 Save the photo

Click Save/Print>Save>Save.

You're ready to print the photo, save it as an Acrobat file, save it in a slide show, or export it into another format to send it via e-mail or display it on the Internet or your personal Web page.

5 Variations

Drive your sister nuts by using the Sphere filter to make her face fatter

Lower your *risqué* factor

The Smudge tool produces an interesting effect when you drag between two contrasting colors. For example, try using it to make flames.

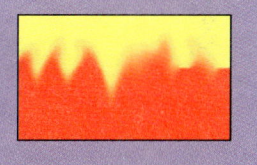

Landscaping your yard

Building, buying, or renovating a house can be a long, costly, and frustrating experience. Here's a quick way to bring your dream back into focus. Spend a little time designing the landscape that now exists only in your mind and put it on paper. It won't make the work go any faster, but it will give you something to look at while you wait.

As with any creative endeavor, landscape design is a process of trying things out, rearranging elements, and changing your mind. Using layers as you create gives you the freedom to add, delete, reject, improvise, and modify—all without changing the original photo.

This example uses trees created in Adobe PhotoDeluxe, but you can just as easily use trees from clip art or stock photos. The landscaping was put on one layer, the paint job on another, and the improvements to the house on a third. To find out how the trees were created, see the tip at the end of the technique.

Landscaping your yard   179

1 Open and save the landscape elements

Open the photo or clip art you're going to use for the trees, bushes, grass, flowers, and so on, and select the elements you want to use for the landscaping.

Click Get Photo>Open File.

Click Modify and choose a selection tool from the pop-up menu in the Select palette. Select the areas you want to use and delete the background from the images if necessary. You want to end up with isolated selections on transparent backgrounds. In this example the tree and bush were saved in the Hold Photo folder.

Click Save/Print>Save>Hold Photo.

2 Open the house photo and add the trees

You probably have a photo of the house you want to landscape. If you don't, quickly draw yourself a house. (Hint: Use the Rectangle tool to draw the house front and the Polygon tool to make triangles for the second-story rafters.)

Click Get Photo>Open File.

Special Effects

Click the Hold Photo bar to display the contents of the Hold Photo folder. Drag the photo, select the photo and click the Paste Layer button, or double-click the photo to add it to the open window.

When you release the mouse button, the Make Layers dialog box appears. Name the layer and click OK. The new layer appears on the top of the Layers palette and the photo appears in the middle of the window.

Use the Move tool to drag the tree into place.

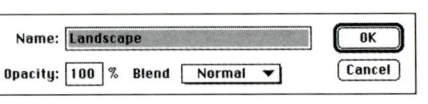

Add as many trees as you want. In this example a second tree was dragged from the Hold Photo folder, resized, and added to the photo. A bush was also added.

When all the elements are in place, click None in the Select palette to deselect the last element.

3 Fix up the house

In this example the landscaping lost some of its impact when it was placed in front of a construction site. To get the full effect, the house was spruced up following the steps in "Filling selections" on page 101. The painting was done on a separate layer. The Landscape layer was turned off while the painting was done.

After the house was painted, the Painting layer was dragged between the House layer and the Landscape layer and all the layers were turned back on.

In this example a driveway and grass were added to complete the picture. The Polygon tool was used to draw the driveway, which was then filled with a gray gradient fill.

The Polygon tool was also used to draw in the lawn area, which was filled with green.

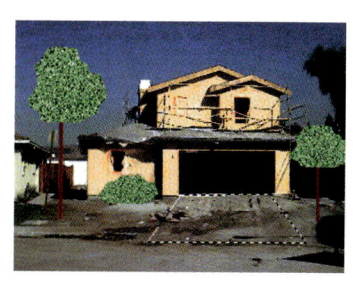

4 Save the photo

Click Save/Print>Save>Save.

You're ready to print the photo, save it as an Acrobat file, save it in a slide show, or export it into another format to send it via e-mail or display it on the Internet or your personal Web page.

When you save an Adobe PhotoDeluxe file, you often merge the layers. In this case you might want to keep the layers, so that you can easily modify the landscaping as the house progresses.

182 Special Effects

Here's a quick summary of how the trees were created in Adobe PhotoDeluxe.

A new file was created. The Trace tool was used to draw the tree-top shape, which was filled with black. Next the Noise and Soften filters were applied to add texture to the leaves.

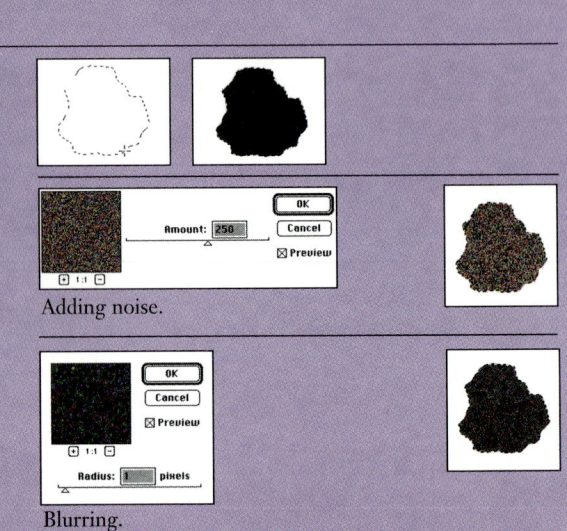

Adding noise.

Blurring.

The color was created by increasing the contrast, removing the saturation, and shifting the color balance.

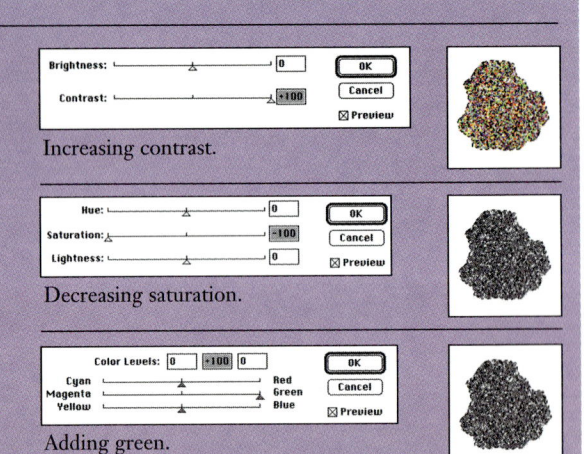

Increasing contrast.

Decreasing saturation.

Adding green.

The Rectangle tool was used to draw the trunk, which was filled with brown.

The trunk was erased to create the bush.

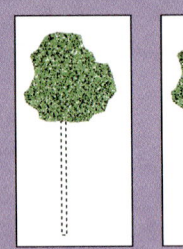

Creating abstract textures

Instead of trying to fix a background or replace a background with another photo, you can often add interest to an image by placing the people or objects against an abstract texture. Textures are also useful for filling shapes, for creating borders, or as stand-alone art pieces. With the application of an Adobe PhotoDeluxe filter, almost anything can become an instant texture.

Filters are the fantasy world of Adobe PhotoDeluxe. It's hard to run out of adventures when you're applying filters to all or part of an image, combining colors and patterns, or piling one filter on top of another. Working with filters comes perilously close to being both an addiction and a mind-altering substance.

Adobe PhotoDeluxe comes with a large number of built-in filters, and many other third-party filter plug-ins are available at your computer store. For more information about plug-ins, see "Creating a kaleidoscope effect" on page 159.

In this example a drawn shape was laid over a gradient fill and then the Ripple and Pond Ripple filters were applied. This technique gives you just a small taste of the fun you will have with filters and other plug-ins.

You don't have to create your own textures. There are many CD-ROMs available that contain hundreds of ready-to-use patterns and textures. You can find textures that run the gamut from natural surfaces, such as wood, metal, and rock, to far-out three-dimensional stereograms.

Special Effects

1 Create a new file and fill it with a gradient

Create a new file that's slightly larger than the background or object you want to fill. If you're not sure what you're going to use the texture for, make a square. You can always make it bigger or smaller.

> You don't normally want to increase the size of an image in Adobe PhotoDeluxe, because enlarging a photo can make the image blurry. This isn't so critical when you're creating an abstract design.

Choose File>New.

Enter a name.

Enter dimensions.

Enter a resolution to fit your printer.

Click OK to create the file.

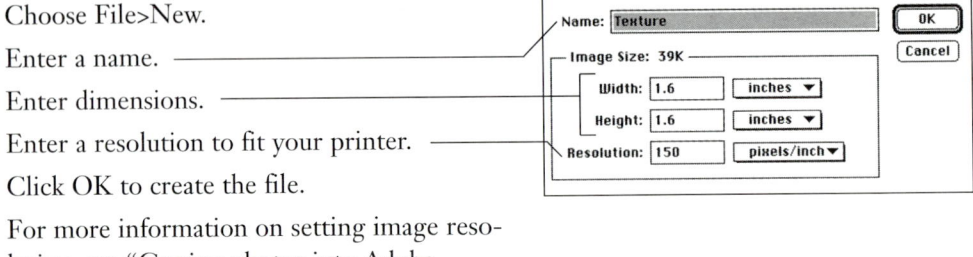

For more information on setting image resolution, see "Getting photos into Adobe PhotoDeluxe" on page 5.

To begin the texture, create a background. You can start with a photo, a solid fill, a pattern, or a gradient. This example uses a gradient as the jumping-off point. You must have a selection before you can apply a gradient fill. In this example the entire image was selected using the All button.

Click Modify>Effects>Gradient Fill.

Click and select a start color.

Click and select an end color.

Click to fill what's selected.

Click a direction. (In this example the start color appears at the left and the end color appears at the right of the selection.)

Click OK to fill.

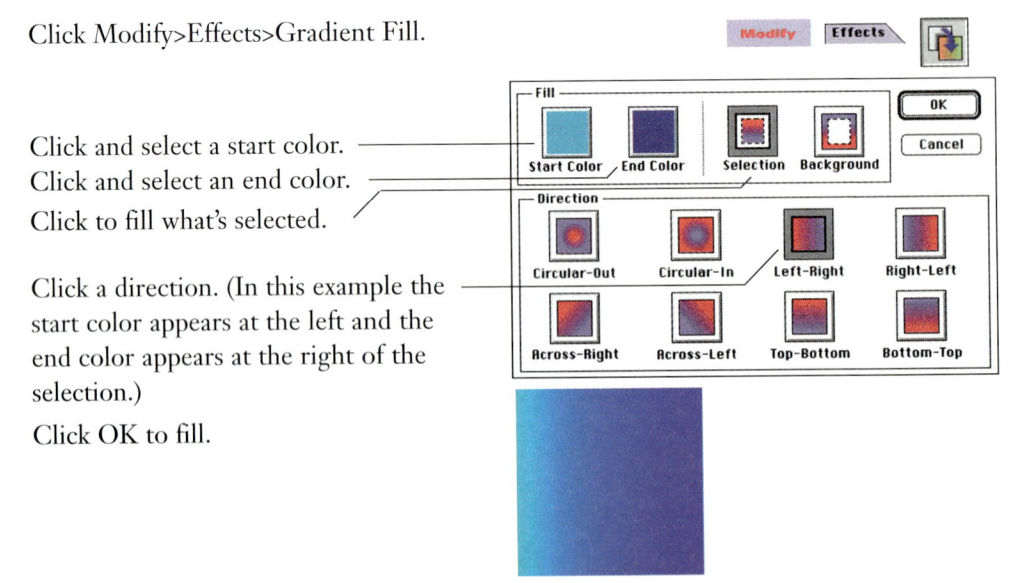

Creating abstract textures 185

2 Draw a shape and fill it with a contrasting color

The shape you draw serves as the selection area. By filtering a selection, you leave the rest of the background untouched. Of course, you can apply the filter to the entire image.

You can use any of the select tools except the Color Wand to draw a shape. If you want sharp corners, use the Polygon tool. If you want repeating shapes, use the Rectangle, Square, Circle, or Oval tool. In this example the Trace tool was used to make a freehand drawing.

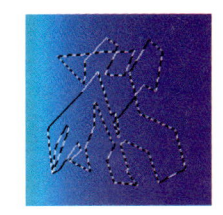

You can get some interesting effects by simply applying a filter to the selection. But for really unusual textures, you need contrasting color. You can fill the shape with a solid color, use the paint tools to paint in color, or use another gradient. In this example the selection was filled using a second gradient.

3 Apply one or more filters

Now let yourself go—try all the filters and combinations of filters. Many filters have dialog boxes in which you can adjust settings. Each one is different, but you'll find them easy and fun to use.

Ripple filter applied

Try changing the filter settings or applying the same filter twice using different settings. Apply the filter to just the selection or to the entire image. Go crazy!

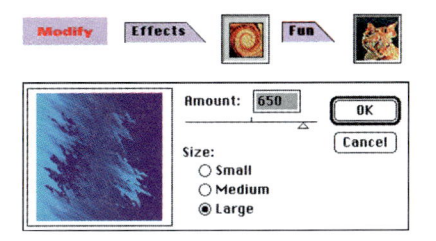

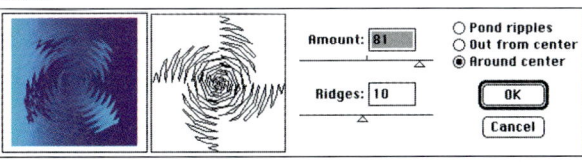

Pond Ripple filter applied

186   Special Effects

4 Save the photo

Click Save/Print>Save>Save.

You're ready to print the photo, save it as an Acrobat file, save it in a slide show, or export it into another format to send it via e-mail or display it on the Internet or your personal Web page.

5 Variations

Mezzotint
(selection only filtered)

Wind
(white selection, feathered)

Shear
(gradient fill in selection)

Ripple
(solid fill, painted lines)

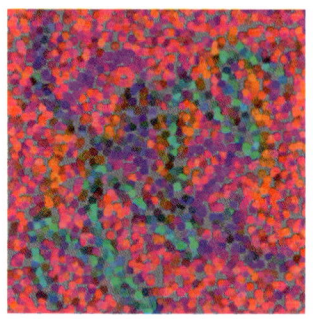

Pointillize

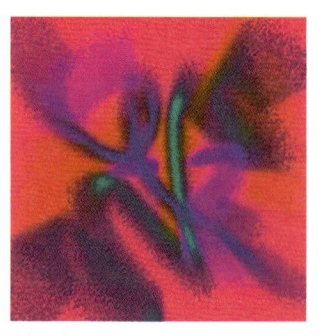

Blur, Zoom option

Creating abstract textures

When you create a new file, the ruler units are always inches. You might prefer to work in a different measurement, such as pixels or picas. You can change the units for a single file or for all future files. To change units for a single file, choose a new unit from the pop-up menu in the New dialog box. To set a new default unit of measurement, choose File>Preferences>Units, then choose a new unit from the Rulers pop-up menu in the Units Preferences dialog box.

Try painting a background instead of using a fill as the basis for a texture. You can also paint lines or shapes instead of filling them. Text can also produce some weird textures.

To add another dimension to textures, you can duplicate filtered selections on different layers and then change the layer opacity or blend settings for the layers.

When you're filling with different colors and gradients, you often find that you want to start over. To clear a selection, press the Delete key on your keyboard. The selection is made transparent. If you want to clear the entire window, click All in the Select palette, press the Delete key, and then click None in the Select palette.

Adding a drop shadow

It's rare that photos contains shadows (at least intentionally), and so they often appear flat and two-dimensional. With Adobe PhotoDeluxe you can add depth to images several different ways. The one you'll probably use the most is the **drop shadow.** Drop shadows work especially well on simple shapes and text, but you can apply a drop shadow to any shape you can select.

There are two ways to add drop shadows: Quick and Dirty (using the Drop Shadow button) and Takes Longer But Is More Elegant (putting a feathered selection on a layer). This technique shows you how to do both.

Another way to add depth to an image is to use the KPT Glass Lens filter. This filter makes your object look like it's reflected in a spherical mirror, complete with reflected shadows. Combining this filter with your own drop shadows presents endless possibilities.

This example takes the technique one step further by applying the filter and the drop shadow to a spherical shape

Adding a drop shadow 189

1 Open the file that contains the object

This example uses an abstract pattern as the starting point for the drawn sphere, but you can use a real object (just apply the Sphere filter), or you can use a shape from clip art. For more information about creating textures, see "Creating abstract textures" on page 183.

To create this sphere the abstract texture was opened and the Circle tool used to draw the shape. The rulers were turned on (View>Show Rulers) to help center the selection tool.

To add dimension to the circle, the KPT Glass Lens filter was applied and the background was deleted.

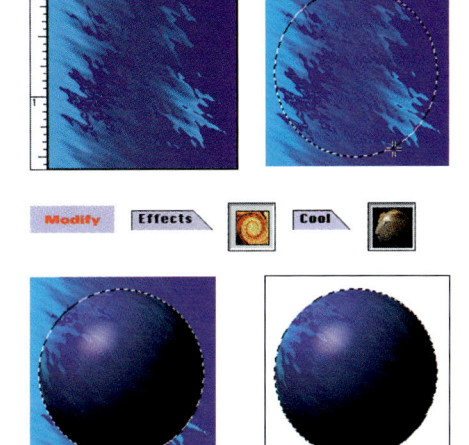

2 Create the simple drop shadow

Using the "instant" drop shadow, you can select a size, a direction, and a color for the drop shadow. Because Adobe PhotoDeluxe creates a new layer that contains both the shape and the shadow, you cannot change or move the shadow after it's created.

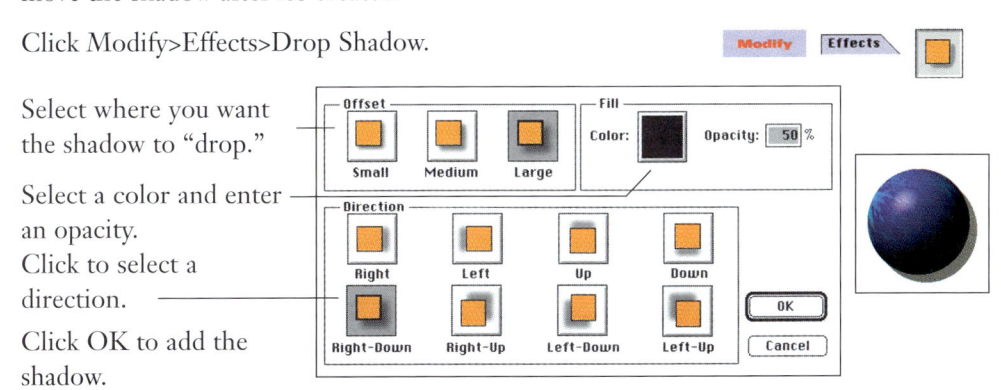

Click Modify>Effects>Drop Shadow.

Select where you want the shadow to "drop."

Select a color and enter an opacity.
Click to select a direction.

Click OK to add the shadow.

3 Create a more complex drop shadow

This simple shadow conveys the effect, but there is a way to get more control over the size and placement of the shadow. To do this, you need to put the shadow on its own layer. To experiment with this method of creating a drop shadow, delete the first drop shadow (if you've created one) and return to the object with no shadow. Delete the background again if necessary and invert the selection so that you end up with the object selected. Use the Darken blend on the new layer for a more realistic effect.

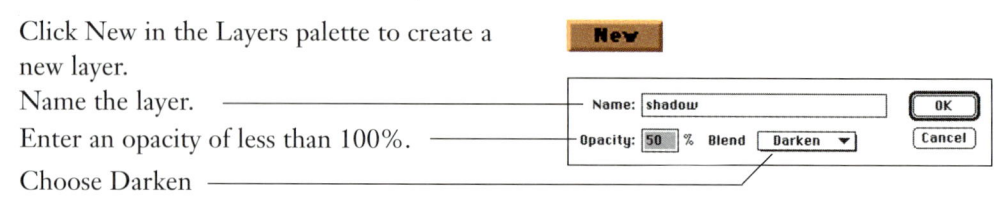

Click New in the Layers palette to create a new layer.

Name the layer.

Enter an opacity of less than 100%.

Choose Darken

Click OK to create the layer.

You should see the selection border on the new layer. (If necessary, go back to the first layer and select the object, then return to the Shadow layer.) To create a soft edge around the drop shadow, which gives it a realistic look, you need to feather the shadow shape as you fill it.

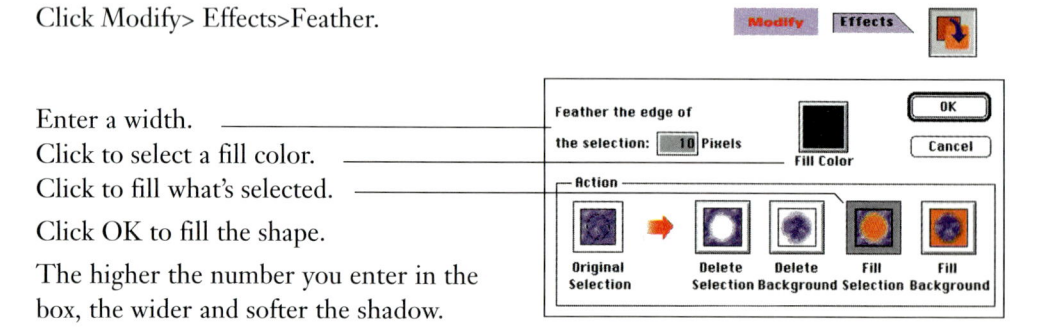

Click Modify> Effects>Feather.

Enter a width.

Click to select a fill color.

Click to fill what's selected.

Click OK to fill the shape.

The higher the number you enter in the box, the wider and softer the shadow.

The result looks murky because the gray filled layer is on top of the sphere. To return the sphere to its former brilliance, drag the Shadow layer under the sphere layer in the Layers palette.

Adding a drop shadow 191

Be sure the Shadow layer is active, then use the Move tool to drag it. To be realistic, match the shadow to your light source; to be unrealistic, create whatever weird light reflections you like.

4 Save the photo

Click Save/Print>Save>Save.

You're ready to print the photo, save it as an Acrobat file, save it in a slide show, or export it into another format to send it via e-mail or display it on the Internet or your personal Web page.

5 Variations

Add type using the Sphere filter

Add a shadow to complex shapes

Create underwater shadows

Special Effects

You can change the direction of the light source for the KPT Glass Lens filter. To move the light source, press a number key as you click the KPT Glass Lens button. 0 makes the light come from behind and 5 puts the light in the center. Try them all.

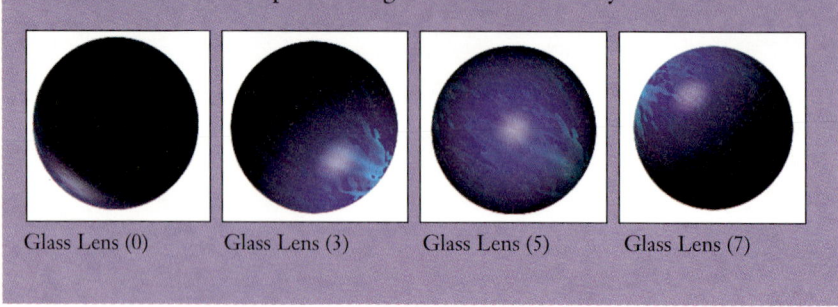

Glass Lens (0)   Glass Lens (3)   Glass Lens (5)   Glass Lens (7)

Changing orientation and perspective

hanging your perspective means looking at things a little differently and sometimes encountering a new reality. Changing a photo's perspective can range from a subtle twist to a wildly unlikely vision. One thing you can be sure of—changing a photo's perspective has an effect on your perspective too!

Perspective determines how close or far away you perceive an object to be. By making part of a photo bigger, you trick the viewer into thinking that something is in a different location. Changing the perspective also introduces some distortion. Using this distortion cleverly is the key to creating an eye-catching photo.

In this example the image was duplicated, its orientation was flipped, and the perspective was altered to produce a three-dimensional effect. If you're going for the three-dimensional look, be sure the original photo isn't too large or you won't be able to print it on a standard piece of paper. Also, changing orientation and perspective requires more memory than other Adobe PhotoDeluxe actions, so keep the photo small. If you find that you're having memory problems, try reducing the photo size or applying the effects to part of the photo at a time.

Special Effects

1 Open and save a copy of the photo

Open the photo you're going to use in the final image. Edit the photo if necessary. While the photo is open, note its dimensions. You will need to know the photo size so that you can create the file for the final image. Then copy the image or selection to the Clipboard. If the photo is very large, or if you're combining photos, save them in the Hold Photo folder.

Click Get Photo>Open File.

Click the size box to find out the photo dimensions.

In this example the entire photo was used. The photo is about 3 x 2 inches. Modify>Edit>Copy was used to store the photo on the Clipboard. No selection was necessary because when nothing is selected, Adobe PhotoDeluxe copies the entire image.

2 Create a new file and paste in one copy

To have room to duplicate the photo and play with its perspective, you need a file that is approximately 2.5 times bigger than the original photo. This photo was about 3 by 2 inches, so the new file dimensions were 7.5 by 5 inches. Make sure to leave enough width to overlap the copies and enough height to stretch the photos edges.

Choose File>New.

Enter a name.

Enter a width and height.

Enter a resolution to fit your printer.

Click OK to create the file.

For more information on setting image resolution, see "Getting photos into Adobe PhotoDeluxe" on page 5.

Paste in two copies of the photo from the Clipboard. (The two will appear one on top of the other.) If the photo is in the Hold Photo folder, click the Hold Photo bar and drag two copies of the photo to the open window.

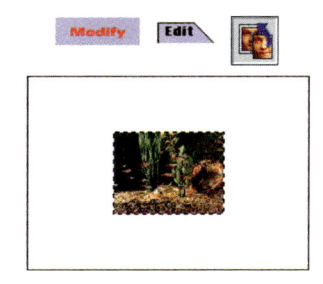

3 Change the orientation and drag into place

Now you're ready to begin building the view-o-rama. First you change the orientation of the top copy of the photo to make up the right side of the final image.

Click Modify>Orientation>Flip Horizontal.

In this example flipping the photo made the fish swim in the reverse direction.

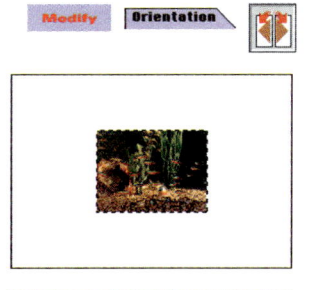

Drag the top copy to the right until the edge of the photo is lined up with the right edge of the window.

4 Change the perspective

Here's where you start shaping a new reality. To get the three-dimensional effect, the edges of the photo nearer the viewer were made larger, so that the smaller center of the image seems farther away.

Click Modify>Size>Perspective.

Drag one of the handles to the top or bottom of the window
To change the perspective, click inside the box with the OK cursor. To cancel the change and try again, click outside the box.

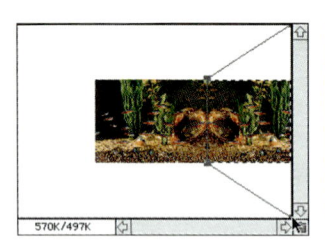

Repeat steps 3 and 4 to complete the 3-D effect shown in the following illustrations.

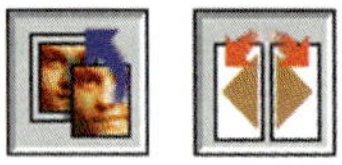

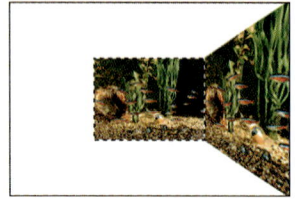

Paste a copy and flip    Drag into position

Change the perspective    Deselect

Changing orientation and perspective

5 Go all the way

Just for fun, try adding a ceiling and floor to the image. Follow the same steps, except click Modify>Orientation> Flip Vertical when you're changing the orientation. You'll need to play with the sizing and perspective until you get an effect you like.

6 Save the photo

Click Save/Print>Save>Save.

You're ready to print the photo, save it as an Acrobat file, save it in a slide show, or export it into another format to send it via e-mail or display it on the Internet or your personal Web page.

7 Variations

Creating a complex collage

Using Adobe PhotoDeluxe, you can produce any fantasy you want—a dream body, a beautifully landscaped yard, a trip around the globe, or even perfect children! Remember, however, that more complex images require more layers, more layers produce larger files, and larger files require more storage space and more internal memory during editing.

To make the most efficient use of your time and your computer's capabilities, make a few notes before you begin working on a complex image. Jot down the order for creating layers and note when you can merge layers during the process.

Here's a sample plan for this collage:
- Open, edit, and save the boy photo in the Hold Photo folder.
- Open the bird photo and delete the background (Layer 0).
- Drag the boy from the Hold Photo folder and erase the background (Layer 1).
- Create a new layer and draw the halo (Layer 2).
- Store the angel in the Hold Photo folder.
- Open the forest (new Layer 0).
- Select and click Paste Layer to move the angel from the Hold Photo folder (new Layer 1).
- Save and merge layers.

1 Open, select, and save the collage pieces

Open the photo or photos that you're using in the collage, select the areas you want to use, and delete the background if necessary. Make any other editing changes and then save the photo or photos in the Hold Photo folder.

Click Get Photo>Open File.

In this example the original photo was cropped using the Trim button and then saved in the Hold Photo folder. The background was not deleted before saving because in this case it was easier to edit the background after combining the image with the bird.

Click Save/Print/Save>Hold Photo.

2 Create the first collage

This technique creates two collages. The first is the bird/boy combination, which was created and then stored in the Hold Photo folder. The second is the bird/boy combined with the forest. To create the first collage, you open the background photo, edit if necessary, and combine the collage elements.

Click Get Photo>Open File.

In this example the bird photo was opened and the Color Wand was used to select the sky. The sky was then deleted.

When you're working with several layers, it's a good idea to give them names so you can distinguish them easily. Double-click the layer in the Layers palette to rename a layer. This layer was named Bird.

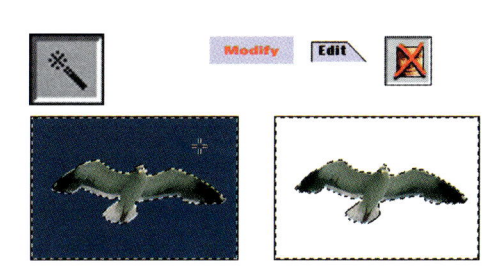

The boy was then laid over the bird photo to produce the angel effect.

Click the Hold Photo bar to display the contents of the Hold Photo folder. Drag the photo, select the photo and click the Paste Layer button, or double-click the photo to move it to the open window.

When you release the mouse button, the Make Layers dialog box appears. Name the layer and click OK. The new layer appears on the top of the Layers palette and the photo appears in the middle of the window.

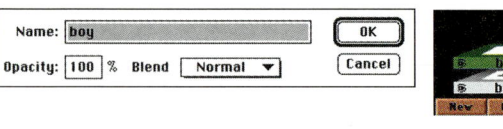

To eliminate the scene behind the boy, the eraser tool was used on the Boy layer. The bird is on a separate layer, so erasing on the Boy layer didn't affect the bird photo.

When you're erasing to clean up a selection, zoom in for a better view, and use small strokes so you can undo if you stray over an area you want to keep.

In this example some editing was done on the bottom layer as well. The Bird layer was activated and erased to clean up stray tail feathers.

Creating a complex collage 201

As a final touch, this winged creature was given a halo. A new layer was created for the drawing. The last active layer was the Bird layer, so the new layer appeared above that layer. (New layers are always added above the active layer.) Before drawing the halo, the new layer was dragged to the top of the Layers palette so that the halo could be sized to the boy's head.

Click New to create a layer. Name the layer and click OK. Then drag the layer to the correct position in the Layers palette.

The Oval tool was used to draw the halo. The halo was outlined with a 3-pixel border to add color and make it thicker.

The collage was then saved in the Hold Photo folder.

3 Create the second collage

To complete the complex collage, continue to open photos and add elements. Adobe PhotoDeluxe can have up to six layers. If you need more layers, merge as you go along. To complete the collage in this example, the angel needed to be placed in his forest home.

Click Get Photo>Open File.

The background photo for this collage didn't need any editing, so the next step was to add the photo from the Hold Photo folder.

Click the Hold Photo bar to retrieve the saved photo. Select the photo and click the Paste Layer button to add the image to the open window (this merges the existing layers in this photo).

When you release the mouse button, the Make Layers dialog box appears. Name the layer and click OK. The layer appears on the top of the Layers palette and the photo appears in the middle of the open window.

Special Effects

Use the Move tool to drag the photo into position.

4 Save the photo

Click Save/Print>Save>Save.

You're ready to print the photo, save it as an Acrobat file, save it in a slide show, or export it into another format to send it via e-mail or display it on the Internet or your personal Web page.

5 Variations

> When you're working with complex images, save often. Not only does this prevent you from having to recreate steps, it also allows you to use the Revert to Last Saved command. With this command you can you backtrack to the last saved version of a file. This can be a lifesaver when you make a mistake after doing several edits. You must save frequently, however, to use this command to advantage.

> Cursors normally appears as cross hairs **(precise cursors).** You can change the cursor so that it resembles the tool you're using. Precise cursors generally work best when you're doing fine drawing or selecting intricate areas, but the other cursors are fine for most situations. You can also change the painting cursors so that they show the size of the brush you're using. To change the cursors, choose File>Preferences>Cursors and select options in the dialog box.

Combining different-sized photos

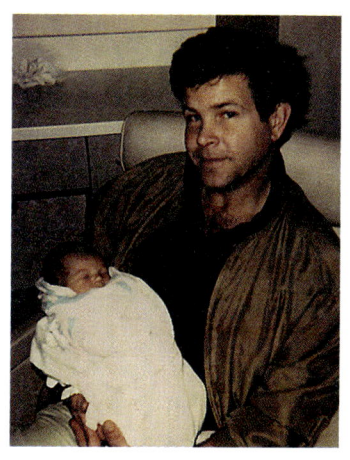

When you're creating a collage and all the pieces are about the right size and the same resolution, it's a simple process to combine them. When the photos you want to use (or the parts you want to combine) are radically different in size or are of different resolutions, putting them together can result in odd size discrepancies. This is fine if you want to create a visual pun, but it can be a challenge when you want to create a realistic image.

One way to overcome the size discrepancies is to put the photos on separate layers and then resize just one layer. This has an advantage over resizing a selection on a single layer because you can resize several times and move the layer frequently, without leaving any holes in the underlying image. Also, you can use the layer opacity setting to make sure the resized selection is the right size, before making the change permanent.

Adobe PhotoDeluxe always converts the photo you paste to the size and resolution of the open window (the photo you're pasting into). To avoid blurriness, copy a higher-resolution photo or larger image into a lower-resolution photo or smaller image. For example, if you have a photo with a resolution of 72 ppi and a photo with a resolution of 200 ppi photo, copy the 200 ppi photo into the 72 ppi photo. The 200 ppi photo or selection may appear very large, but you can reduce its size without affecting the quality of either image.

Special Effects

1 **Open the larger or higher-resolution photo and save it in the Hold Photo folder**

When you're combining photos, you should always reduce the size (or resolution) in Adobe PhotoDeluxe. Open the photo you plan to reduce and save it in the Hold Photo folder. That way it will have its own layer when you bring it into the final image.

Click Get Photo>Open File.

In this example the money bag is larger than the new dad. (It also happens to be a higher resolution.) The Color Wand was used to select the background and the background was deleted. The photo was then stored in the Hold Photo folder.

This example uses a checkerboard to display the transparent areas on a layer. See "Displaying transparent areas of a layer" on page 23 for more information.

Click Save/Print>Save>Save to store the photo.

2 **Open the smaller or lower-resolution photo and add the saved photo**

This is the photo that determines the size and resolution that you want to make the copied photo or selection.

Click Get Photo>Open File.

Click the Hold Photo bar to display the contents of the Hold Photo folder. Drag the photo, select the photo and click Paste Layer, or double-click to add the photo to the open window.

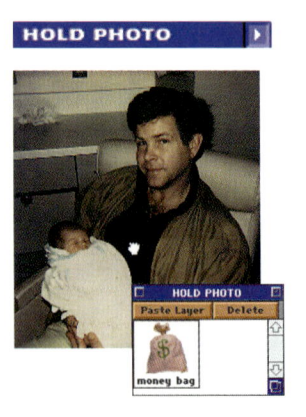

When the Make Layer dialog box appears, enter an opacity of less than 100% so you can use the underlying photo to guide the placement of the pasted photo.

Enter a name.
Set the opacity at less than 100%.
Leave the blend at Normal.
Click OK to make the layer.

The new layer appears in the Layers palette and the photo appears in the middle of the window. In this case it almost obscures the underlying photo.

3 Resize and edit the photo

Because the photo is on its own layer, you can move it close to its final location, resize, move again, resize again, and so on.

In this example some overlap was left after resizing, so that the money bag could be tried out in a few locations and still cover the entire blanket. The excess was removed later.

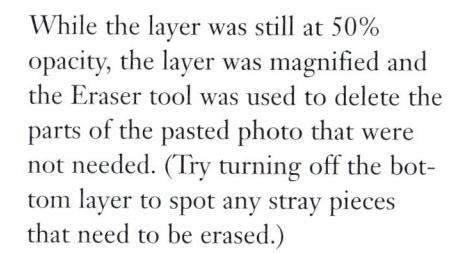

While the layer was still at 50% opacity, the layer was magnified and the Eraser tool was used to delete the parts of the pasted photo that were not needed. (Try turning off the bottom layer to spot any stray pieces that need to be erased.)

The layer opacity and magnification was returned to 100% to produce the final image.

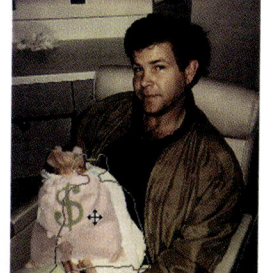

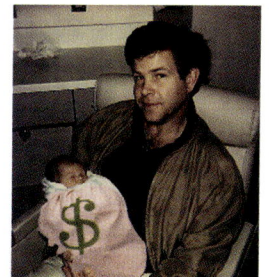

4 Save the photo

Click Save/Print>Save>Save.

You're ready to print the photo, save it as an Acrobat file, save it in a slide show, or export it into another format to send it via e-mail or display it on the Internet or your personal Web page.

5 Variations

Creating a brochure or report cover

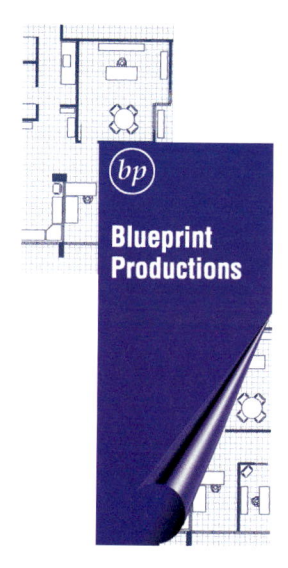

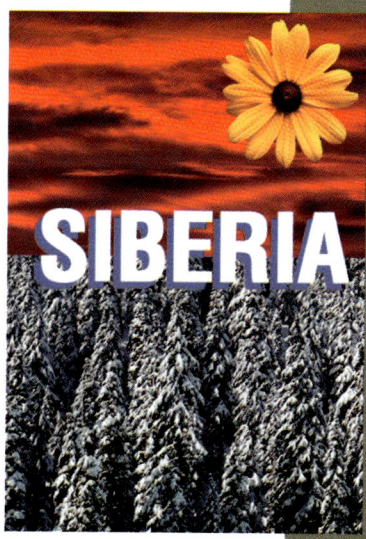

When you're trying to reach potential clients for your home-based business, you often have to compete with bigger companies that have many more resources. You can use Adobe PhotoDeluxe to design a brochure that expresses personal, one-on-one service, without costing you a week's profits.

You can design the finished brochure yourself and print it on your own printer or at a copy center. If you're going to produce the brochure in large quantities, or if you want high-quality four-color output, create a mock-up in Adobe PhotoDeluxe and take it to a service bureau. You can work with the people there to refine the final layout and choose the printing colors.

You can also use Adobe PhotoDeluxe to design presentation and report covers. There are a million interesting ways to combine photos, text, and special effects. You can be sure that your unique creation will make a lasting impression on your clients or teachers.

This technique uses a solid-color background, simple text, and a plug-in filter from Kai's Power Tools. The KPT Page Curl filter adds a nice touch to any type of document cover. A second piece of art was used to fill in the curled-back section. The report cover was created using art from the Adobe PhotoDeluxe Samples folder

Special Effects

1 Open and save the cover elements

If you're going to add photos or other art to your cover, you need to save the art elements before you begin creating the cover itself.

When you apply the Page Curl filter, the area under the curl is filled with gray. If you want to paste a photo or piece of art into this area, you need to save it before creating the brochure cover. Make sure the art is big enough to overlap the space a bit so you can drag it around once it's pasted.

If your cover requires only one photo or piece of art, you can save it to the Clipboard. If you're combining more elements, save them individually in the Hold Photo folder.

Click Get Photo>Open File.

In this example a section of a blueprint was scanned. The art was copied to the Clipboard instead of saved in the Hold Photo folder because it didn't need to be on its own layer in the final image.

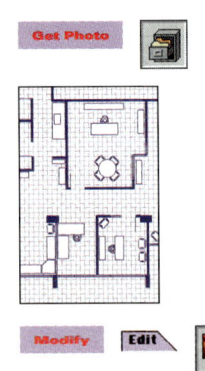

Click Modify>Edit>Copy to copy to the Clipboard.

2 Create the brochure cover

Your cover can be a photo, a photo on a color background, a piece of art, or just about anything else that fits a brochure's dimensions. In this example a new file was created and filled with a solid color and then text and a logo were added.

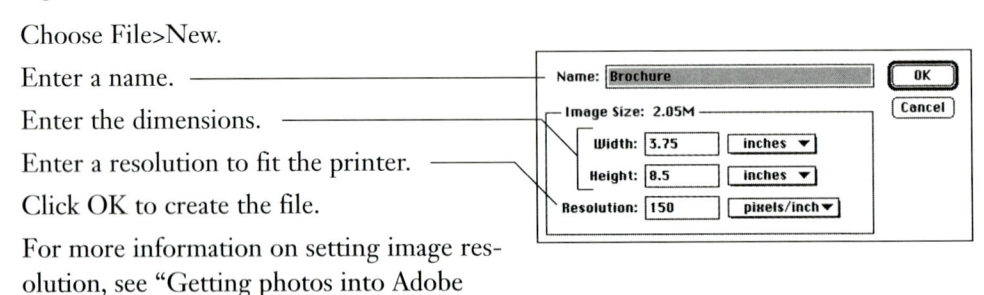

Choose File>New.

Enter a name.

Enter the dimensions.

Enter a resolution to fit the printer.

Click OK to create the file.

For more information on setting image resolution, see "Getting photos into Adobe PhotoDeluxe" on page 55.

Creating a brochure or report cover 209

The background was then filled with a color to simulate the color of the paper the brochure would be printed on.

Click Modify>Tools>Color Change.

A deep blue was selected from the Color Swatches palette to provide the background color.
This design uses two pieces of text in slightly different fonts and sizes to distinguish the company logo from the company name. A small circle draws attention to the logo.

To add text, click Modify>Tools>Text.

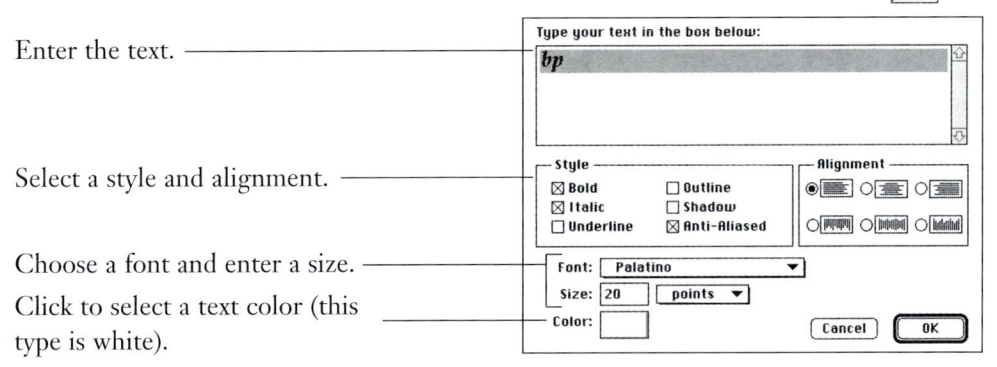

Enter the text.

Select a style and alignment.

Choose a font and enter a size.

Click to select a text color (this type is white).

Click OK to enter the text.

A text layer is added to the Layers palette and the text appears in the middle of the window. Click None to deselect the text so you can see it without the selection border, then use the Move tool to drag the layer until the text is in the right place.

In this design the logo looked a little lost in a sea of blue. To make it stand out, the Circle tool was used to enclose the text.

The border of the circle was then outlined with a pixel width of 3 to make it thicker.

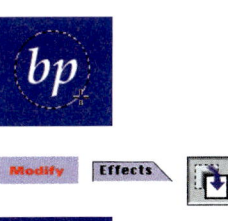

The company name was added using a different font and size.

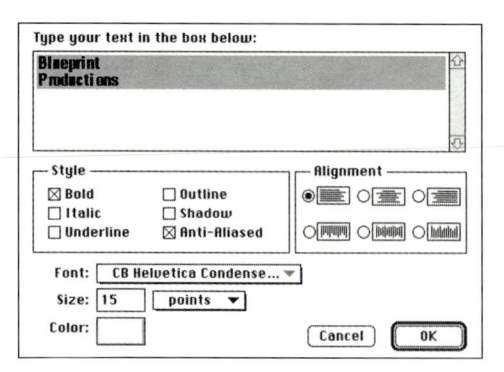

The text was deselected and dragged into place using the Move tool.

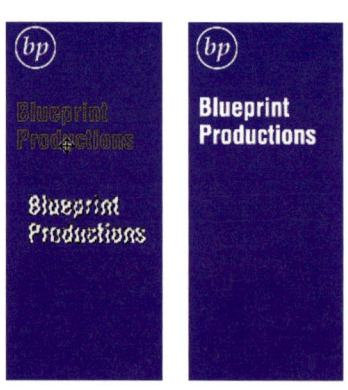

3 Add the page curl

How or if you apply the Page Curl filter is up to you. You can curl the entire page or just a selection. You can fill the resulting space or leave it blank. You'll probably want to experiment before making your final choice.

Click Modify>Effects>Special Effects> Cool>KPT Page Curl.

For this brochure the lower right corner of the page was selected using the Rectangle tool and the filter was applied. The curled area is automatically filled with gray.

The Color Wand was then used to select the gray area and the art on the Clipboard (which was copied in Step 1) was pasted in. If you need to reposition pasted art, drag the selection.

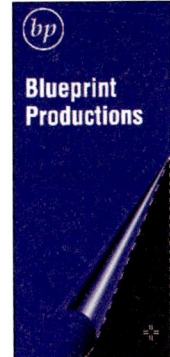

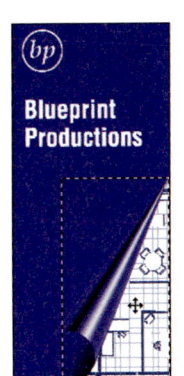

4 Save the photo

Click Save/Print>Save>Save.

You're ready to print the photo, save it as an Acrobat file, save it in a slide show, or export it into another format to send it via e-mail or display it on the Internet or your personal Web page.

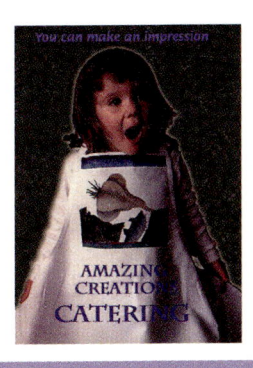

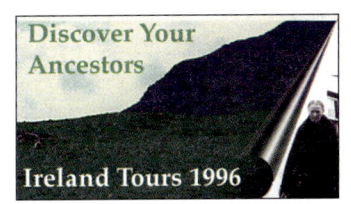

5 Variations

With the Page Curl filter you can change the location of the curl. By default, the lower right edge of the image or selection curls. To change the curl, press a number key as you click the Page Curl button.

- Press 1 to curl from the lower left corner.
- Press 7 to curl from the upper left corner.
- Press 9 to curl from the upper right corner.

Creating cartoons

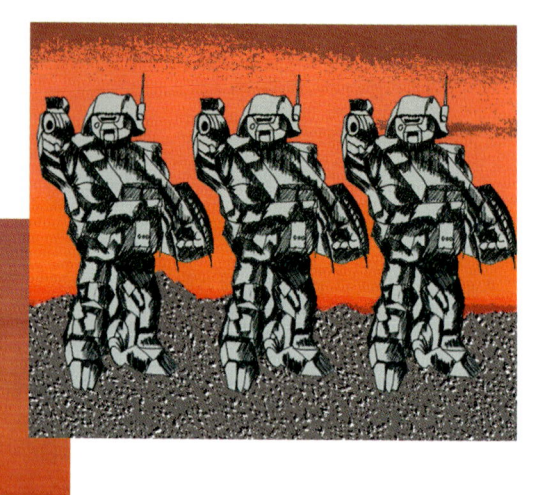

Much of the time you spend playing with Adobe PhotoDeluxe will be spent working with photographs— fixing colors, replacing backgrounds, restoring missing pieces, creating collages, trying out effects, and so on. But be sure to save some time to delve into the world of pure fantasy and imagination.

The cartoon in this technique started with a drawing and took off from there. You can make your own drawing in an illustration program or use a character from clip art. The rest of this scene is pure Adobe PhotoDeluxe magic. You can use any combination of photos, art, and filters to visit your alternative world. Adobe PhotoDeluxe layers are the perfect way to try out different outer-space scenarios while still keeping your passage back home open.

In this example the black-and-white art was colorized. The sunset background was posterized to reduce it to a few stark colors, then the alien soil was produced using a combination of filters. Finally, the single invader was turned into a rapidly growing force.

Creating cartoons 213

1 Open, edit, and save the cartoon character

Decide which photo, texture, or piece of art will be the background image to which you'll add the elements. Open any other files and edit them if necessary. Because you will want to bring each of them in on its own layer, save the elements in the Hold Photo folder.

Click Get Photo>Open File.

In this example the figure's white background needed to be deleted before he was stored in the Hold Photo folder. Before selecting, the layer transparency display was changed to a checkerboard, making it easier to differentiate the deleted background from the original opaque, white background. For more information about setting layer transparency, see "Displaying transparent areas of a layer" on page 23.

The Color Wand was used to select the background and the background was then deleted, leaving the figure on a transparent background.

To add some dimension to the figure, its contrast was lowered to give it more of a sketched appearance. To complete the edit, some color was added to the figure.

Click Modify>Quality>Brightness/Contrast.

Drag the slider to adjust the contrast.

Click OK to change the contrast.

There are several ways to add color to this figure. One of the easiest is to try out combinations in the Color Balance dialog box.

Click Modify>Quality>Color Balance.

Drag the sliders to add or subtract colors. (In this example adding blue and subtracting red resulted in a purple hue.)

Click OK to change the color.

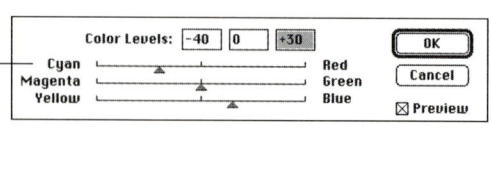

With the editing complete, the figure was stored in the Hold Photo folder.

2 Open and edit the background photo

The possibilities for manipulating any image are endless. This example used an approach requiring multiple filters. By varying the settings in the filter dialog boxes, you could play this game for hours.

Click Get Photo>Open File.

The background in this example was posterized to reduce the number of colors in the photo. Posterizing produces large area of flat color that provide strong contrast with reduced detail.

Click Modify>Effects>Special Effects>Artistic>Posterize.

Enter the number of colors.

Click OK to posterize.

Click Done when you're ready to leave the Special Effects area and return to the other Modify buttons.

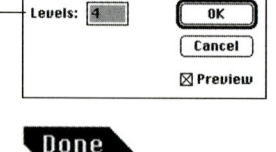

Creating cartoons 215

In this example the figure is larger than the sunset, so the background needed to be increased in height to accommodate the drawing. The canvas was increased to make the photo higher.

Click Modify>Size>Canvas Size.

Enter new dimensions. (In this example the canvas was increased by about 1 inch.)

Click where you want the photo to appear in relation to the new canvas. (In this example the photo appears in the top middle of the canvas.)

Click OK to increase the canvas.

When you add canvas it is transparent (and probably appears as white in the image unless you've got transparency set to appear as a checkerboard).

The Rectangle tool was used to select the new canvas. The selection was filled with black using the Color Change button and then deselected.

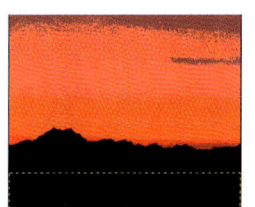

The Color Wand was used to select the enlarged black area. Two filters were applied to give texture to this area.

The Grainy Dots option in the Mezzotint dialog box was used for this effect.

The Emboss filter on the Effects>Stylize menu was used for this effect.

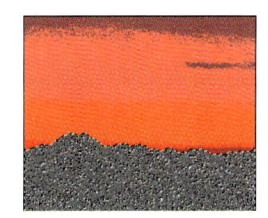

3 Add the figures

Click the Hold Photo bar to display the contents of the Hold Photo folder and move the photo into the open window.

The figure was dragged from the Hold Photo folder three times to create three separate layers. Then the layers were dragged with the Move tool to arrange the figures.

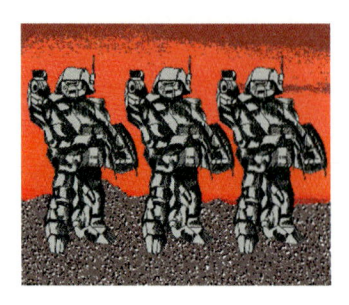

4 Save the photo

Click Save/Print>Save>Save.

You're ready to print the photo, save it as an Acrobat file, save it in a slide show, or export it into another format to send it via e-mail or display it on the Internet or your personal Web page.

5 Variations

The Posterize filter can produce amazing results. The lower the number you enter for the levels, the starker the image. Higher numbers produce more subtle effects.

Using hidden bonus filters

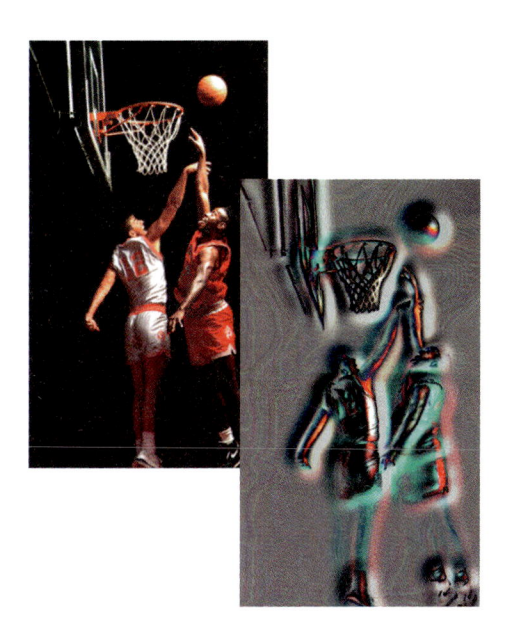

Adobe PhotoDeluxe is a powerful yet flexible program that you can use in many different ways. You decide how to combine the tools, buttons, and effects to get your own unique images. You also have a choice of how you select those tools and effects. Some people like to make their choices by clicking buttons and selecting tools; others prefer to make choices from menus. How you use Adobe PhotoDeluxe is up to you.

There's a special bonus for exploring the Adobe PhotoDeluxe menus. The Effects menu contains several filters that don't have button counterparts in the graphical interface. These filters can add yet another dimension to your creativity. Try them alone or in combination with the filters in the Special Effects section.

To use the filters found only in the menus, you must turn on Long Menus. For more information about using long menus and keyboard shortcuts, see "Using menus" on page 27. In this technique the filters were chosen from the Effects menu.

Special Effects

1 Open the photo and duplicate the layer

Edit and color correct your photos before you try out filters. When you get a version that you like, save it and then start experimenting with a copy of the file.

Click Get Photo>Open File.

Click Modify>Edit>Copy to copy the photo to the Clipboard.

You could just apply the filter to a single-layer photo, but you can produce a more dimensional effect that has more detail by applying the filter to a duplicate layer that has been created with the Difference mode. To see a 3-D effect, you view the original and the filtered layers together.

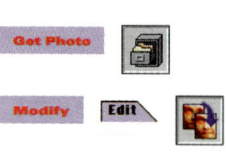

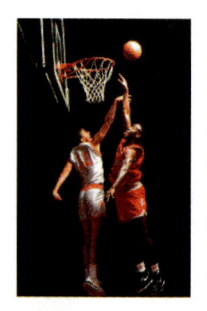

Click the New button in the Layers palette to create a layer.

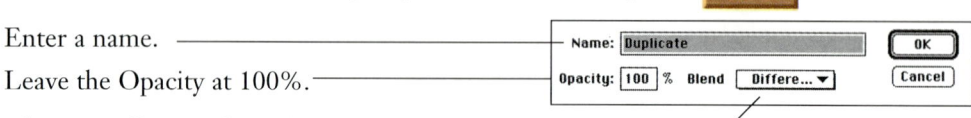

Enter a name.

Leave the Opacity at 100%.

Choose Difference from the Blend menu.

Click OK to create the layer.

Click Modify>Edit>Paste to paste the photo from the Clipboard.

If you try this, don't panic! The Difference blend makes the photo look entirely black. Just turn off the bottom layer to see the layer you're working on. Once you make some changes to the duplicate layer, the bottom layer adds detail to the photo.

Using hidden bonus filters 219

2 Apply a combination of filters

To create a memorable image, you can apply any filter or combination of filters. The secret is to experiment with filters and filter settings until you find some you like. When you're experimenting with a bunch of filters, it's a good idea to jot down the filter settings when you change them in a dialog box, so you can reproduce the effect. (Filter dialog boxes keep the last settings until you change them.)

In this example the action shot was softened to blur the sharpness and produce a dreamy effect.

Choose Effects> Special Effects>Blur> Soften.

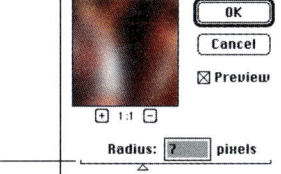

Drag the slider to indicate how much blur you want.

Click OK to blur the photo.

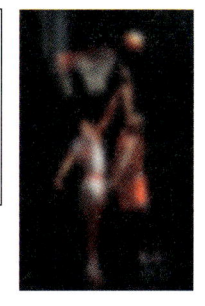

Another filter was used to outline the edges where the color changes in the photo.

Choose Effects>Special Effects>Artistic> Find Edges.

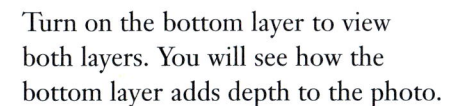

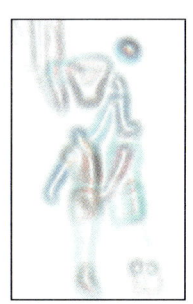

Turn on the bottom layer to view both layers. You will see how the bottom layer adds depth to the photo.

Special Effects

As a final touch, the photo was embossed.

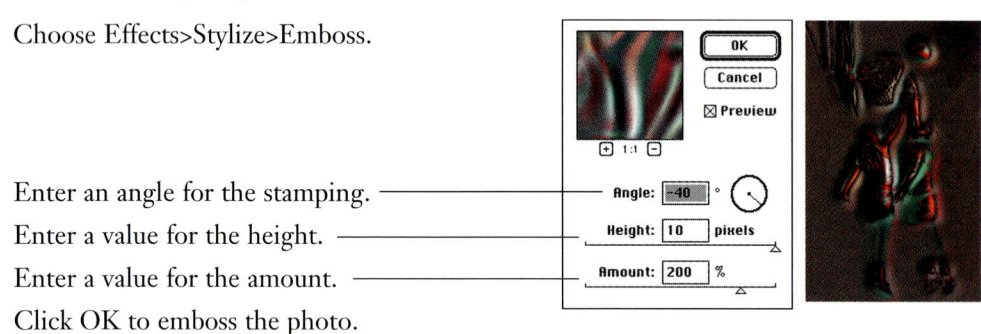

Choose Effects>Stylize>Emboss.

Enter an angle for the stamping.

Enter a value for the height.

Enter a value for the amount.

Click OK to emboss the photo.

3 Save the photo

Click Save/Print>Save>Save.

You're ready to print the photo, save it as an Acrobat file, save it in a slide show, or export it into another format to send it via e-mail or display it on the Internet or your personal Web page.

4 Variations

Here are some other filters that you'll find on the Effects>Stylize menu.

Original photo

Facet filter

Fragment filter

Diffuse filter

Emboss filter

Trace contour filter

Sometimes when you're applying filters it's useful to adjust the brightness or contrast as you go along. This helps brings out highlights and details in the filtered images. Click Modify>Quality> Brightness/Contrast to adjust these settings. In this example the brightness and contrast were individually adjusted to +50.

Why not just keep the photo on the bottom layer, apply the filters to different layers, and then turn the layers on and off to see the results? The secret is that you have to have something on a layer in order to apply a filter. To filter an image, you have to copy and paste it to a layer before applying a filter.

SECTION 5

Save, Print, and Store Photos

Once you've created your Adobe PhotoDeluxe masterpieces, what do you do with them? This section explains how to save your photos so you can print them, display them on your computer screen, share them with others, and use them in other applications.

There are lots of things you can do with your photos besides printing them on paper. You can save them in a screen-saver slide show, and you can send them to your friends and family on electronic mail. You can also display your photos on a personal Web page or on one of the many Internet sites that showcase user art.

Your main reason for using Adobe PhotoDeluxe may be to edit your photos for use in memos, newsletters, or brochures. In that case, you'll probably want to put them in a word-processing or page-layout program, such as Home Publisher or Adobe PageMaker.

One of the benefits of digital images is that they don't lose their quality, even after they've been stored for years. No color fading, no spilled coffee, no torn edges—and best of all, no lost negatives. This section concludes with some storage tips to help you keep your photos in order so you can find them when you want them.

Saving photos   224

Exporting photos   227

Printing photos   231

Putting photos online   233

Using Adobe PhotoDeluxe photos in other applications   235

Storing photos   236

Saving photos

There are two different aspects to saving photos. There's the saving you do as you work in a photo, to keep your changes and prevent screaming fits and hair tearing when an unexpected power failure occurs. Then there's the saving you do when you're finished editing a photo. Each type of saving requires a different approach in Adobe PhotoDeluxe.

Saving while you work

Adobe PhotoDeluxe opens and saves all photos in the Adobe PhotoDeluxe **file format,** which automatically preserves all the layers in your photo. To save a file, click Save/Print>Save>Save. The first time you save, you're asked to name the file. It's a good idea to save at least every 15 minutes when you're working on a project.

If you want to save a *copy* of your photo as you go along (perhaps to try out variations) choose File>Save As from the menu and then enter a new name or store the photo in another location. The copied file appears in the Adobe PhotoDeluxe window.

Saving a finished photo

Many of the photos you edit in Adobe PhotoDeluxe end up having layers. These layers are necessary while you're working on the photo, but once you're finished you have the choice of saving the file with its layers or merging the layers and saving a **flattened** (single-layer) file. A file with layers is larger than one with a single layer, so layered photos take longer to print, take up more disk space, and take more time to send online and for others to download. In most cases maintaining layers is not useful. When you're sure you're not going to change a photo again, merge the layers before you save it. (Only the Adobe PhotoDeluxe and Photoshop 3.0 file formats can save layers. If you save in any other format, the layers are lost anyway.)

Adobe PhotoDeluxe merges only **visible** layers—that is, layers that have their eye icon turned on. Once you've merged layers, they're gone—you can't separate the layers again.

To merge layers, click the Delete button at the bottom of the Layers palette.

Select to merge layers.
Click OK to merge.

Once the layers are merged, save the single-layer file just as you would any other Adobe PhotoDeluxe file.

Saving a photo as an Adobe Acrobat file

Adobe PhotoDeluxe can save your file as an Adobe Acrobat file, which can be opened by anyone who has the Acrobat Reader. (A free copy of the reader that you can share with others is included on the Adobe PhotoDeluxe CD-ROM.) The viewer doesn't need to have the same kind of computer you do, or have Adobe PhotoDeluxe or another graphics program, to look at your photo. Acrobat is a good format choice for photos you're sending electronically or displaying on the Web.

To save a file in Acrobat format, click Save/Print>Save>Create Acrobat File. Adobe PhotoDeluxe saves the file in the Portable Document Format (PDF). Layers are not preserved when you save a photo in Acrobat format. For more information on creating Acrobat files for online use, see "Putting photos online" on page 233.

Saving photos for a screen-saver slide show

Using Adobe PhotoDeluxe, you can create your own on-screen slide show, which you can display as a screen saver when you're not using your computer. The slide show runs as part of the After Dark® screen-saver application. A free, limited version of this application is included on the Adobe PhotoDeluxe CD-ROM. You must install After Dark before you can run the slide show. The After Dark Installation folder is automatically installed on your computer when you install Adobe PhotoDeluxe. To install After Dark, locate the folder and double-click to start the Slide Show Installer.

To save a file for the slide show, click Save/Print>Save>Screen Saver Slide Show. The Slideshow/Screen Saver dialog box appears. Photos are saved in PICT format and layers are not preserved.

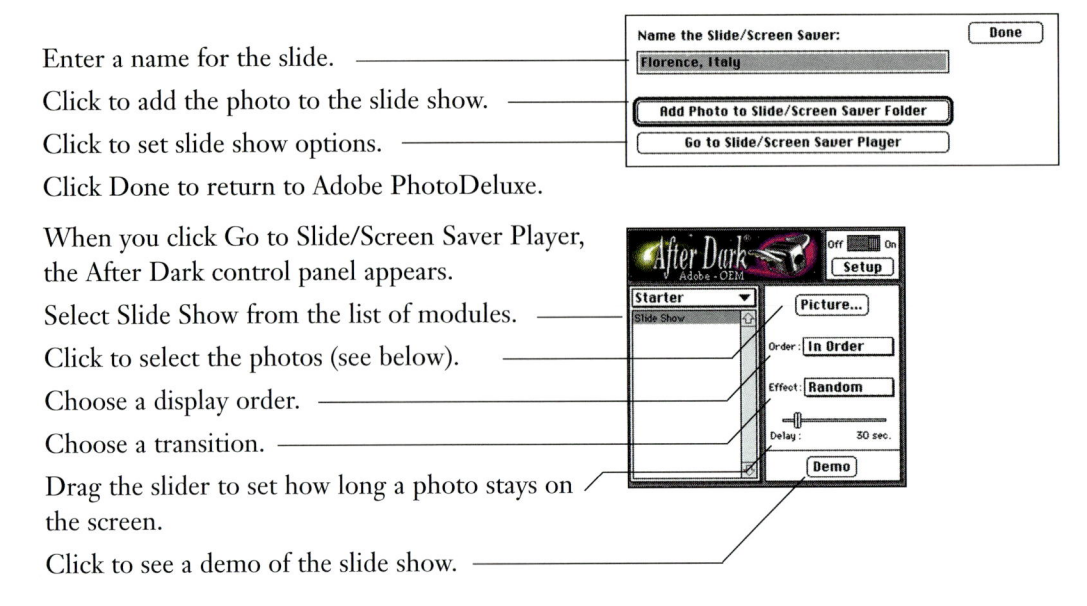

Enter a name for the slide.

Click to add the photo to the slide show.

Click to set slide show options.

Click Done to return to Adobe PhotoDeluxe.

When you click Go to Slide/Screen Saver Player, the After Dark control panel appears.

Select Slide Show from the list of modules.

Click to select the photos (see below).

Choose a display order.

Choose a transition.

Drag the slider to set how long a photo stays on the screen.

Click to see a demo of the slide show.

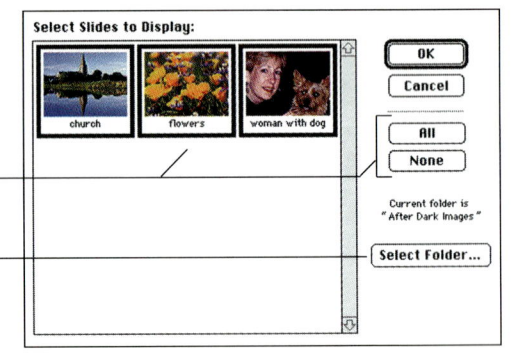

When you click Picture in the After Dark control panel, After Dark displays the photos you've saved for the slide show.

Select the photos you want to include, or click All or None.

If necessary, click Select Folder and move to the folder where you've stored the photos for the slide show.

Click OK to return to the After Dark control panel.

To delete a photo from the slide show, locate the file in the Finder and drag it to the trash.

Exporting photos

When you want to use an Adobe PhotoDeluxe photo in another application, send the file to someone via e-mail, use the photo on a Web page, or give the photo to someone who has a different kind of computer, you **export** the photo. Exporting saves the photo in a format other than the Adobe PhotoDeluxe file format.

To export a file, choose File>Export>File Formats (unless you're saving the file in GIF format; in that case choose File>Export>GIF 89a). The Export dialog box appears.

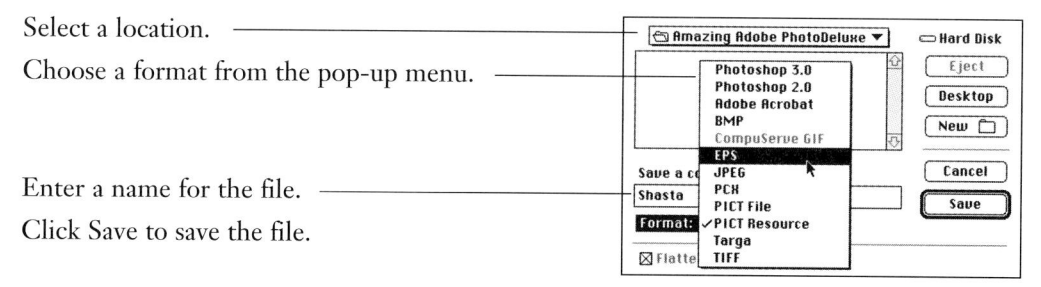

Select a location.

Choose a format from the pop-up menu.

Enter a name for the file.

Click Save to save the file.

The table on the following page shows the available file formats and when you might use each one. For specific instructions on saving files in EPS, JPEG, and GIF formats, see the sections following the table.

Exporting in EPS format

EPS files are used by many illustration and page-layout programs. You can save a preview of the file in Macintosh (PICT or JPEG) or TIFF format. Choose TIFF if you're using the photo on an IBM-compatible computer. Previews give you an idea of what the picture will look like and let you place the image in the illustration or on the layout page.

To save the file, choose File>Export>File Formats and then choose EPS from the Format menu. The EPS dialog box appears.

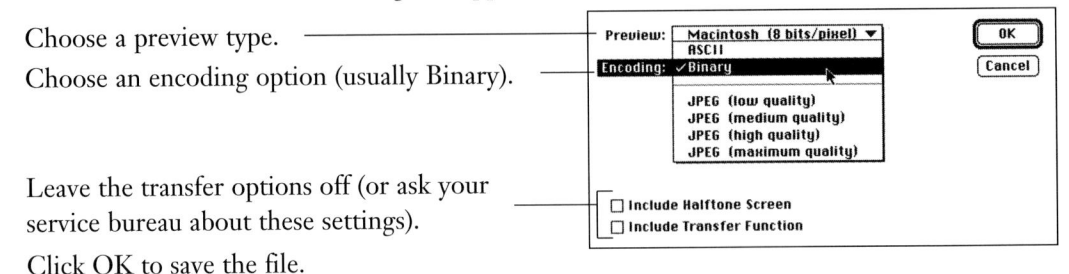

Choose a preview type.

Choose an encoding option (usually Binary).

Leave the transfer options off (or ask your service bureau about these settings).

Click OK to save the file.

Leave the Encoding option at Binary unless you know that the application you're using can't accept binary files. To compress an EPS file as you save it, choose a JPEG option from the Encoding menu.

Exporting in JPEG format

The JPEG format compresses your Adobe PhotoDeluxe file by identifying and discarding the extra data that is not essential to the display of the photo. In most cases you can't tell the difference between the original photo and the compressed photo.

You have four quality choices when you compress a photo using JPEG. The Maximum setting produces the best quality image and results in the largest file size. The Low setting produces the least quality image and results in the smallest file size. JPEG files are automatically decompressed when they're opened.

To save a the file using JPEG, choose File>Export>File Formats and then choose JPEG from the Formats menu. The JPEG dialog box appears.

Select a quality option.

Click OK to save the file.

File Format	Uses	Notes
Photoshop 3.0	Working with files in PhotoShop 3.0	This is the same file format as Adobe PhotoDeluxe. Saves layers.
Photoshop 2.0	Working with files in PhotoShop 2.0, 2.5, or applications that support only 2.0 or 2.5 files	Saves the file in Photoshop 2.0 format. Merges layers.
Adobe Acrobat	Sending files to others who don't have Adobe PhotoDeluxe or publishing on the Web	Saves the file in PDF format. Has the same effect as clicking Save/Print>Save>Create Acrobat File.
BMP	Saving files to be used on DOS and MS/Windows-compatible computers	In the dialog box, select Microsoft Windows or OS/2 format and indicate a bit depth.
EPS	Including files in an illustration or page-layout program such as Adobe Illustrator or Adobe PageMaker	See "Exporting in EPS format" on page 229 for information on setting EPS options.
JPEG	Compressing files	See "Exporting in JPEG format" on page 229 for information on setting JPEG options.
PCX	Saving files to be used on DOS and MS/Windows-compatible computers	
PICT File	Including files in Macintosh graphics and page-layout applications or as an intermediary file format for transferring files between applications	PICT format is especially effective for compressing images that contain large, flat areas of color.
PICT Resource	Using the file as a startup screen or including the file as a PICT resource in an application program	
Targa	Using files on systems that use the Truevision video board (supported by some MS-DOS color applications)	In the dialog box, select a resolution (in bit depth).
TIFF	Transferring files between applications and computer types	In the dialog box, select the Macintosh or Windows format. To compress as you save, click LZW compression.

Exporting in GIF format

GIF (graphics interchange format) is used to display images on Web pages and online services. With the GIF file format, you can define the parts of the image that you want to be transparent and select a transparency color for the Web browser. (When you leave an area transparent, it floats on the background. For example, you might want to display just the outline of a head instead of having the head inside of a color rectangle.) GIF format also lets you reduce the total number of colors in the image to create a smaller file that is displayed and downloaded more quickly.

You use Adobe PhotoDeluxe layers to create the transparent areas. To prepare the photo, select the area you want to include, if you're not using the entire photo. Copy and paste that selection to a separate layer. Hide the original layer and any other layers that you don't want to include.

Original photo

Selection on transparent layer

To save the file in GIF format, choose File>Export>GIF89a Export. The GIF dialog box appears. Select the option you want to use, as described next.

Selecting a transparency color. Click the color box to select a color for the transparent areas. (To make the transparency the same color as the Web page background, leave it at the default gray setting.)

Choosing a palette. Choose Exact from the Palette menu if your photo contains 256 or fewer colors. This option uses a palette that displays the file in true-to-life colors. If your photo contains more than 256 colors, choose the Adaptive palette for the best results. The Adaptive option creates a palette from the most commonly used colors in the image. You can use the System palette to display the photo, but this option can produce unexpected results when the image is displayed on an 8-bit monitor using a different built-in palette.

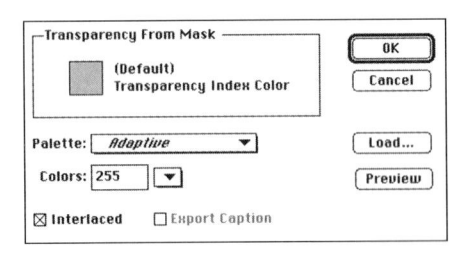

Reducing the number of colors. If you choose the Adaptive palette, type a number in the Colors text box or choose the number of colors from the Colors pop-up menu. Experiment until you have the smallest number of colors that still keeps the detail you want in the photo. To check how the photo will look in the Web browser with the selected number of colors, click the Preview button in the GIF dialog box. Click OK to return to the GIF dialog box.

In this small photo with few colors, reducing the colors doesn't change the file size much. In a larger photo, or one with many colors, reducing the number of colors can significantly reduce the file size.

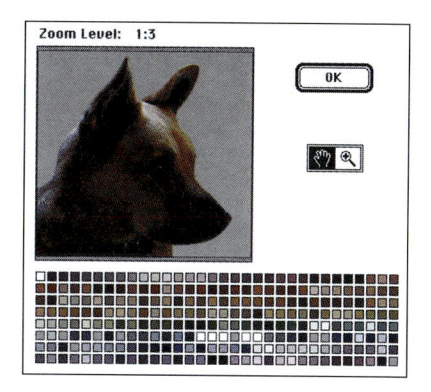

255 Colors, 165k   32 Colors, 83k

Choosing a download method. Leave the Interlaced option selected if you want the image to be displayed gradually during downloading. Interlacing displays increasingly higher resolution detail as a photo is downloaded. Deselect the Interlaced option if you're using the photo as a background or texture, so that it's downloaded all at once.

Click OK in the GIF dialog box to save the file in GIF format. Adobe PhotoDeluxe automatically assigns a .gif extension to the file name.

Printing photos

You can print your Adobe PhotoDeluxe photos on your own desktop printer, or you can take them to a copy center for printing. Most of your photos will look best when printed in color, but you can print Adobe PhotoDeluxe photos on a grayscale printer. Depending on the resolution of your printer, printing in grayscale can cause you to lose some of the photo's subtlety, because some colors will become muddy and others will appear as pure black or pure white with no detail. To print in grayscale or black and white, choose the appropriate option in the Print dialog box.

The smaller the file the faster it prints. The fewer the number of layers, the smaller the file. If you're experimenting with a photo collage and want to see a printed version, make a copy of the file and merge the layers. When you're ready to edit again, return to the layered file.

Adobe PhotoDeluxe prints only visible layers. Turning layers on and off is another way to temporarily reduce the file size for printing. See "Viewing layers" on page 22 for more information on visible and invisible layers.

When you're working in On Your Own, you have three print choices. Click Save/Print> Print and then click one of the following buttons.

Displays the set-up options for your printer. Select your usual options.

Displays a preview of how the photo will look on the page (the page reflects the size setting in the Page Setup dialog box).

Displays the print options for your printer. Select your usual options.

When colors don't match

Sometimes when you print your photos, the colors don't match the ones you see on the screen. This is because color monitors display color by adding the colors together and reflecting the resulting color back to your eye (red + green = yellow). Printer paper, on the other hand, absorbs the printing ink and displays color by subtracting one color from the other and reflecting the nonabsorbed color back to your eye (cyan + magenta - yellow = green). If you find that you're not getting the colors you want in your printed photos, you can use a color management system (CMS), such as Kodak Precision Color. A CMS lets you set up your monitor and your printer so that they work together to produce the same colors in your screen display and your printed output.

Putting photos online

> No matter how you use your photos onscreen—as part of a slide show, attached to or embedded in an e-mail message, or displayed on a Web page, there's one rule that applies to all situations:
>
> **Online files should be as small as possible.**

Photos for screen-saver slide shows

When you're collecting photos for a screen-saver slide show, you want the slides to be as small as possible to conserve disk space. Your photos are going to be displayed on the screen, so there's no point in using photos with resolutions higher than the 72 ppi or 96 ppi resolution of your screen. You should also keep in mind the dimensions of your monitor. Don't make the physical dimensions of the photo bigger than your screen (or the screen that the slide show will be shown on). For more information, see "Changing the size and resolution of a photo" on page 25.

Photos for slide shows are saved in the PICT format. Adobe PhotoDeluxe automatically saves in this format when you click the Screen Saver Slide Show button. Photos must be in this format to appear as a screen saver, so you can't make your slide-show photos smaller by saving them in JPEG or Acrobat format.

If you have room on your hard disk, or if you want to edit the photo in the future, make a copy of the photo for the slide show. Then you can change the size or resolution and save the photo in the screen-saver format, which merges all layers, without worrying about your original photo. For more information, see "Saving photos for a screen-saver slide show" on page 225.

Photos for electronic mail

Sending photos to friends and relatives online is one of the greatest pleasures of using Adobe PhotoDeluxe. However, no one wants to spend a lot of time sending or receiving files—even Grandma has been known to grow impatient with waiting more than a few minutes! Keep your electronic files small. Unless the person on the other end is going to print the photo, don't make the resolution higher than the monitor can display (72 ppi for the Macintosh,

96 ppi for Windows machines). If the file will be printed, it probably needs a resolution of 150 or so.

If the person you're sending the photo to has Adobe PhotoDeluxe or another graphics program, save the photo in JPEG format. JPEG compresses the file without losing any of the photo's color or detail. If the recipient doesn't have a graphics program, save the file as an Acrobat file and be sure to include the Acrobat reader from the Adobe PhotoDeluxe CD-ROM. For more information, see "Saving a photo as an Adobe Acrobat file" on page 225 and "Exporting in JPEG format" on page 229.

Photos for Web pages

More and more people are creating their own Web pages on the Internet or adding their photos to collections on other online services such as CompuServe and America Online. It's fun and exciting to see your photos on display and to get comments and feedback from other digital photo fanatics.

As with all electronic transfer and display, you want to keep these files small. It's always a good bet to set the photo resolution to 96 ppi. That way, all users can display the image at or near its actual size (the photo will be slightly bigger on Macintosh monitors that display at 72 ppi). Remember too that the image will appear on many different-sized monitors. Make the photo small enough so that the entire image can be seen on a 13-inch monitor.

You also want to keep the number of colors in the photo to a minimum. Adobe PhotoDeluxe includes the GIF89a format for saving files to use on Web pages, online services, and other Internet sites. The GIF format automatically compresses your file and lets you reduce the number of colors. See "Exporting in GIF format" on page 230 for step-by-step instructions on saving a GIF file.

You can also save files for Web pages using the Acrobat format, which also compresses the photos. The secret to creating an effective Adobe Acrobat file is to keep the file as small as possible, while leaving enough resolution so that the file can be magnified on the screen, or printed, and still maintain its quality. For more information, see "Saving a photo as an Adobe Acrobat file" on page 225.

Using Adobe PhotoDeluxe photos in other applications

Adobe PhotoDeluxe photos are great for viewing on your computer, sending to friends and relatives, putting in Web pages, and using in printed cards, flyers, and invitations. You can also use your photos in many other applications. For example, you might want to include a picture in a letter (one going via the U.S. post office), or put a photo in a newsletter or brochure.

Using your photos in other applications is easy, as long as you save the photo in a file format that can be understood by the other program. See the application's documentation for a list of formats that can be imported into the program. In most cases you choose the Place, Insert, or Import command from the File menu to include a photo in another application.

Unless you're transferring the photo to Adobe Photoshop 3.0, you must save your photo in a format other than the Adobe PhotoDeluxe format. This means that your layers are lost. Use the File>Export command to save photos in other formats.

Here's a quick reference for saving files to use in other applications. See "Exporting photos" on page 227 for a complete rundown on all the file formats you can save in from Adobe PhotoDeluxe.

To use a photo in:	Save the photo as:
Word-processing programs	TIFF PICT (Macintosh) BMP (Windows) PCX (Windows)
Page-layout programs	EPS TIFF
Illustration or drawing programs	EPS TIFF PICT BMP (Windows) PCX (Windows)

Storing photos

There are a few things you should keep in mind as you begin accumulating digital images.

You don't have a negative! You can't go back and recreate an image by having it printed again. This means that the edited copy of the photo on your computer is your one and only original. Be sure to back up your Adobe PhotoDeluxe images.

Digital files are large. It's a good idea to save your photos in JPEG format before you store them. In any case, you're probably going to need more storage space. Floppy disks are fine for giving photos to others, or carrying them to and from the copy center, but if a file is larger than 1.3 MB it won't fit on a floppy disk.

A hard disk is the most reliable (and most expensive) storage medium. There are also removable drives that store data on cartridges. Several inexpensive portable drives are available that store from 25 MB to 100 MB of information—a fair number of photos—on floppy-disk-sized cartridges. Larger removable cartridges are available, with capacities up to 280 MB, but these cartridges and drives are expensive and useful only if you have very large images that you'll be carrying to and from a service bureau.

If you have your photos scanned onto a PhotoCD, you're a step ahead in the storage game, but you'll still need somewhere to store the finished Adobe PhotoDeluxe images. Many copy centers and service bureaus can press a custom CD-ROM of your images, and the prices of recordable CD systems are getting lower all the time. CDs are compact, they can store hundreds of photos, and they keep your computer's memory available for more of your amazing Adobe PhotoDeluxe images.

As you get more and more digital images, you'll need some way to catalog and retrieve them. There are several **browser applications** on the market, such as Adobe Fetch, that can help you organize and access your photos quickly and easily.

Index

abstract textures, 185
Acrobat
    file format for, 28, 225, 228
    Reader, 225
active layer, identifying, 37
Add button, 15
Adobe
    Acrobat. *See* Acrobat
    Fetch, 236
    Illustrator, 97
    PhotoDeluxe. *See* PhotoDeluxe
    Photoshop, file format, 110
    Type Manager, 77
After Dark®, 225–226
aligning text, 48, 49
All button, 13
Anti-Aliased option, recommended, 77
Apple Quick Take™ camera, 6. *See also* digital cameras
art, on CD–ROM, 8, 12
Artistic special effect category, 141
ATM, 77

backgrounds. *See also* layers
    background layer, 37
    creating, with filters, 140–142
    deleting, 39
    diffusing, 89
    feathering, 47
    transparent areas and, 23
black-and-white photos
    adding color to, 86
    converting color photos to, 76, 145 146
    tinting, 72–76

blends, 51–54, 104–105
Blur special effect category, 141, 142. *See also* Noise filter; Soften filter
blurriness, fixing, 35
BMP file format, 228, 235
body parts
    enhancing, 92–95
    hiding, 173–177
    replacing, 168–172
book, how to use, 2–3
borders
    outlining with, 39
    selection borders, 13, 17
brightness, 87–90
brochure covers, 207–211
browsers, for digital photos, 236
Brush tool. *See also* drawing; painting
    creating text with, 50
    described, 17–18
    touch-up with, 59
business cards, 97–100

cameras, digital. *See* digital cameras
canvas size, 43, 107
cartoons, 212–216
CD-ROM
    art stored on, 8
    opening files from, 12
    photos stored on, 7, 236
Circle tool, 14, 189

237

Circular filter, 142, 143
clip art
    adding color to, 68–71
    adding to photo, 152
    overview, 8
Clipboard
    copying selection to, 34
    deciding between Hold Photo folder and, 67
    disadvantage of using, 60
    Export Clipboard option, disabling, 30
Clue Cards, 3, 29
collages, 144–148, 198–202
color
    adding to drawings, 68–71
    balancing, 82–86, 117, 120
    black and white, converting to, 76, 145–146
    in borders, 39
    complementary, 120
    components of, 84
    correcting, 116–120
    in fixing scratches, 33
    matching between screen and printer, 232
    matching within photo, 40
    posterization and, 89
    saving in GIF format and, 230–231
    selecting, 18
    selecting photos by, 14–15
    in text, 48
Color blend mode, 51
Color Change tool, 17, 73–74, 76
color management systems, 232
Color Swatches palette, 18
Color to BW, 76, 145–146
Color Wand
    Change Color button vs., 76
    overview and basic use, 14–15, 47
    tolerance, changing, 15, 93
contrast, 83, 87–90
Cool special effect category, 141
copying
    files, 224
    selections, 17, 34, 132. *See also* Clipboard
copyright, digital images and, 8–9
covers, brochure or report, 207–211
cross hairs, cursor as, 202
cursors, changing, 202

Darken blend mode, 51, 153
decorations files, 12
deleting
    backgrounds, 39
    layers, 24, 167
    selections, 42, 187
depth of field, 59
deselecting selections, 16, 28, 74
Difference blend mode, 54
Diffuse filter, 220
digital cameras
    opening files from, 12
    overview, 6
    scanners as, 121–124
digitizing photos, 5–8. *See also* CD-ROM; digital cameras; scanning
disks
    space needed on, 2, 29, 30
    storing photos on, 236
Distort button, 137

Index

downloading photos. *See* exporting photos
drawing. *See also* Brush tool
   abstract shapes, 185
   grids, 164–165
   on layers, 37–38
   patterns, 130–134
   trees, 182
drawing programs, saving photos for, 235
drop shadows, 188–192
duplicating selections, 17, 132. *See also* copying

editing tools, 17–18. *See also specific tool*
electronic mail, sending photos via, 233–234
Emboss filter, 215, 220
EPS format, 229, 235
Eraser tool, 17, 103
Export Clipboard option, disabling, 30
exporting photos
   basic procedure, 227
   in EPS format, 229
   formats for, list of, 228, 235
   in GIF format, 230–231
   in JPEG format, 229

faces, retouching, 92–96
Facet filter, 220
fair use, copyright and, 9
feathering, 47, 50
Fetch, 236
files. *See also* photos; selections
   flattened, 24, 224
   formats for, 228, 235
   reverting to earlier version, 202
   size of, performance and, 2, 29, 233
filling. *See also* painting
   selections, 38, 101–105
   text, 77–81
filters. *See also specific filter*
   brightness/contrast and, 221
   categories, 141
   creating backgrounds with, 140–142
   image placement on layer required, 221
   overview, 126
   previewing, 91
Find Edges filter, 142
flattened files, 24, 224
flaws, removing, 32–35
flipping selections, 158
floppy disks, storing photos on, 236
fonts, 48, 77
Fragment filter, 220
Free Resize button, 49, 63
Fun special effect category, 141

Get Photo, 12
GIF format, 230–231, 234
Glass Lens filter, 189, 192
gradient fills, 79
graininess, 61–62
Grainy Dots effect, 215
graphic interchange format, 230–231, 234
grids, working with, 163–167

hard disks. *See* disks

Hide Rulers, 28
highlights, in adjusting black and
   white, 83
Hold Photo folder
   disk space and, 110
   overview, 19, 41
   saving and, 28
   using, 42–44
hue, 84, 86

illustration programs
   creating type in, 97
   saving photos for, 235
Illustrator, 97
images. *See* photos; selections
Instant Fix button, 83
Invert button, 16

JPEG format, 229, 234, 236

Kai's Power Tools. *See* KPT
kaleidoscope effect, 161
Kodak
   Digital Camera, 6. *See also* digital
      cameras
   Photo CD, 7. *See also* CD-ROM
   Picture Exchange, 8
   Precision Color, 232
KPT
   described, 159
   Glass Lens filter, 189, 192
   Page Curl filter, 210–211
   Vortex filter, 161, 162

landscaping, planning, 178–182
layers
   active layer, identifying, 37

creating, 21
deleting, 24
drawing on, 37–38
Layers palette, 21
maximum allowed in file, 21
merging, 24, 29
moving, 22
naming, 22
overview, 20, 36
painting on, 37–38, 69
printing and, 231–232
rearranging, 22, 45
saving photos and, 224–225
selecting everything on, 23
tinting photos and, 76. *See also*
   tinting photos
transparent areas of, displaying,
   23
trying out effects via, 111–115
viewing, 22
Lighten blend mode, 51, 73
lightness, as color component, 84
Line tool, 17, 18, 165
long menus, 27–28, 131

magnifying
   photos, 27, 91
   windows, 131
marquees, 13
measure, units of, 187
memory
   amount used by images, 2
   assigning extra to PhotoDeluxe,
      29
   special effects and, 143
   virtual, not recommended, 29
menus, 27–28, 131

merging layers, 24
Mezzotint filter, 134, 215
Modify command, 13
monitors, resolution and, 26
moving
    layers, 22, 81
    selections, 17, 34, 39
    text, 81, 98

naming layers, 22
New button, 15, 37
Noise filter, 61–62
None button, 16, 137
Normal blend mode, 51

On Your Own, 12
opacity
    alternate method for changing, 104
    basic use, 52, 105
    number keys for, 18
opening photos, 12
orientation, 78, 192
outlining photos, 39
Oval tool, 14, 38
overlapping photos, 106–110. *See also* photos, combining
Overlay blend mode, 51, 69

Page Curl filter, 210–211
page-layout programs, saving photos for, 235
Page Setup button, 28
painting. *See also* Brush tool; filling
    on drawings, 68–71
    fixing flaws by, 35

on layers, 37–38
panoramas, 106–110
pasting
    layers (Paste Layer), 19, 108
    selections over selections (Paste), 34, 132
    selections into selections (Paste Into), 62, 63
patterns, drawing, 130–134
PCX file format, 228, 235
PDF file format, 28, 225, 228
perspective, 193, 195–196
PhotoDeluxe. *See also specific component or operation*
    documentation for, 3
    file format for, 224
    taking photos for, tips, 6–7
photos. *See also* selections
    black-and-white. *See* black-and-white photos
    brightness, 87–90
    color in. *See* color
    combining
        basic procedure, 42–45
        into collages, 144–148, 198–202
        different-size photos, 203–206
        different-type photos, 144–148
        into panoramas, 106–110
        showing one through another, 60–63
        with text, 46–49, 135–139
    contrast in, 83, 87–90
    converting to black-and-white, 76, 145–146

Index

digitizing, 5–8. *See also* CD–ROM; digital cameras; scanning
dimensions of, displaying, 139
editing, 42, 43
exporting. *See* exporting photos
feathering, 47, 50
flaws on, removing, 32–35
layers of. *See* layers
magnifying, 27
motion effect in, 126–128
opening, 12
orientation, 78, 192
perspective, 193, 195–196
placement, via Canvas Size dialog box, 153
printing, 28–29, 231–232
putting online, 233–234
resolution. *See* resolution
retouching, 92–96
retrieving, 19
saving. *See* saving
scanning, 5–6
screen saver, putting into, 28, 225–226, 233
selecting entire, 13, 28
selections vs., 13
sharpening, 58, 59, 86
sizing, 25–26, 184
soft focus, 96
space around, adding, 43, 107
taking, tips for, 6–7
tinting, 72–76
using with other applications, 235
Photoshop file format, 110, 228
picas, as measurement unit, 187
PICT file formats, 228, 233, 235

Pinch filter, 175–176
pixels
   described, 4
   moving layers by, 45
   working in, 187
placement grids, working with, 163–167
Pointillize filter, 134, 142
Polygon tool, 14, 181
Pond Ripple filter, 185
Posterize filter, 89, 216
PostScript fonts, 77
previewing
   printouts, 29
   special effects, 91
printing, 28–29, 231–232
public domain, copyright and, 9

Quality (blurring) options, 143

RAM. *See* memory
Reader, Acrobat, 225
Rectangle tool, 14, 83, 143
Reduce button, 13, 15
Remove Dust/Scratch button, 33
report covers, 207–211
Resize button, 25
resolution
   defined, 4
   changing, 25–26
   monitor affecting, 26
   online photos and, 233–234
   photos of different, combining, 203–206
   scanning and, 5–6
   screen saver slide shows and, 233
retouching, 92–96

Index

retrieving photos, 12, 19
Revert to Last Saved command, 202
Ripple filter, 185, 186
rotating photos, 78
rulers, showing and hiding, 27–28

sample art files, 12
saturation, as color component, 84
saving
    basic procedure, 28
    finished photos, 224–225
    formats for, 227–228, 235
    in Hold Photo folder, 28
    recommended frequency of, 28, 202
    for screen saver, 28, 225–226
    under another name, 224
scanners
    described, 4
    opening software for, 12
    using as camera, 121–124
    using with PhotoDeluxe, 5–6
scratch disks, 30
scratches, removing, 33–34
screen saver, putting photos into, 28, 225–226, 233
selections. *See also* photos
    adding to, 15
    borders for, 13, 17
    combining tools for, 16
    copying, 34, 132
    deselecting, 16, 28, 74
    distorting, 137
    duplicating, 17, 132
    filling, 38, 134
    flipping and rotating, 157–158
    inverting, 16
    making, 13–15, 115
    moving, 17, 39, 167
    photos vs., 13
    reducing, 15
Selection Fill button, 38
Select palette, 13
sepia tone, 72
service bureaus, 5
shadows
    in adjusting black and white, 83
    drop shadows, 188–192
    in retouching, 93–94
shapes. *See* Circle tool; Oval tool; Polygon tool; Rectangle tool; Square tool; Trace tool
sharpening photos, 58, 59, 86
Shear filter, 186
Show Rulers, 27–28
silhouettes, 64–67
sizing
    photos, 25–26, 184
    selections, 56–58
    text, 49
slide show, for screen saver, 28, 225–226, 233
Smudge tool, 17, 96, 175, 177
Soften filter, 59, 91, 96
special effects. *See* filters
Sphere filter, 191
Spin (blurring) option, 143
Square tool, 14, 166
stock photos, 8
storing photos and selections
    on CD-ROM, 7, 8
    in Hold Photo folder. *See* Hold Photo folder overview, 236
style, in text, 48

Stylize menu, filters on, 220

Targa file format, 228
teeth, enhancing, 94–95
text. *See also* selections
    adding to photos, 46–49, 100
    as background, 149–153
    filling, 77–81
    fonts, 48, 77
    formatting, 48, 49
    judicious use of, 46
    moving, 81, 98
    showing photo through, 135–139
    sizing, 49
textures, abstract, 185
Threshold setting, 33, 34
TIFF file format, 228, 235
tinting photos, 72–76
tolerance, of Color Wand, 15, 93
tools. *See also specific tool*
    for editing images, 17–18
    for selecting images, 13–18
Trace contour filter, 220
Trace tool, 14, 34
transferring files. *See* exporting photos
trees, drawing, 182
Trim button, 25, 45
TrueType fonts, 77
Turn Off All Clue Cards command, 3
Twirl filter, 156

undoing
    operations, 59, 142
    settings, 100
units of measurement, 187
viewing, layers, 22

vignettes, 74–75
virtual memory, not recommended, 29
Vortex filter, 140, 161, 162

Wind filter, 128, 142
word processors, saving photos for, 235
World Wide Web, putting photos on, 230, 234

Zoom (blurring) option, 143
zooming in and out, 27, 91, 131

About the authors

Kate O'Day has been designing and writing instructional materials for over fifteen years. Kate has created tutorials, user's guides, and online documentation for Adobe Systems, Apple Computer, Ashton-Tate, Claris, Macromedia, and Software Publishing Company.

Kate wrote the *Adobe Photoshop 2.5 User Guide* and the *Adobe Photoshop 3.0 User Guide*. She is also the author of the award-winning *Adobe Photoshop Classroom in a Book*.

Kate has been a photographer for over twenty years and lives in Berkeley, California.

Linda Tapscott has been a graphic artist for over twelve years. Her company, Spitting Image, has designed and produced projects for Adobe Systems, Creative Publications, *New Media Magazine*, McGraw Hill, and other publishers. She has produced covers for *Dr. Dobb's Journal*, *Visual Basic*, and *Database Programming and Design*.

Linda works extensively with Adobe Photoshop and Adobe Illustrator. She was responsible for designing and creating the illustrations for the *Adobe Photoshop 3.0 User Guide*.

Linda lives with her husband in Fremont, California.

The authors would like to express their thanks to

Brendan Collins, Matt Crowley, Ken Culp, Bill Ferry, Meredith Mustard, Shelby Sampson, Brigid, Peanut, Shasta, and Dinah

and at Adobe Systems

Patrick Ames, Bruce Chizen, Melissa Dyrdahl, Pamela Lu, Anjali Magana, Kyle Mashima, Drew McManus, Barry Owen, and Stephanie Schaefer

A very special thanks to

Mary Jane H. Pine

Editor in Chief
Patrick Ames

Editor
Jesse Wood

Cover design
Graham Metcalfe and Paula Shuhert

Book production and cover artwork
Graham Metcalfe

Printer
Shepard Poorman

Typefaces
Body: Janson
Display: Helvetica Condensed

Adobe Press books examine the art and technology of digital communications. Published by Macmillan Computer Publishing, Adobe Press books can be found wherever books about computers and the communication arts are sold.

Scanning resolutions

For the best output on	Use this resolution
Macintosh monitor	72 pixels per inch (ppi)
PC monitor	96 ppi
300 dpi laser printer	100 ppi
600 dpi laser printer	150 ppi
725 dpi inkjet printer	150 ppi
1200 dpi or higher image setter	1.5 times the screen frequency (lpi)*

* Talk to your service bureau for information about producing this very high-quality output.

Opening Photos

When you're working in On Your Own (which you get to from the opening screen of Adobe PhotoDeluxe), you have six choices for opening a digital file. Click Get Photo and then click one of the following buttons.

	Opens a file stored on your hard disk. Adobe PhotoDeluxe opens all files in its own format. If the file you open is in another format, it's opened as an untitled file. The original file is not changed. Click Find and enter the name to locate a file.
	Opens a sample art file. These files are stored on the Adobe PhotoDeluxe CD-ROM. You must have the Adobe PhotoDeluxe CD-ROM in your drive to open one of these files. Click a category, then double-click to open a sample file.
	Opens a decorations file. You need an open file to add a decoration. These files are stored on the Adobe PhotoDeluxe CD-ROM. You must have the Adobe PhotoDeluxe CD-ROM in your drive to open one of these files. Click a category, then double-click to open a decoration file.
	Opens a file that's stored in your digital camera. You must drag the camera's plug-in module into the Acquire/Export folder in the Adobe PhotoDeluxe Plug-ins folder to have it appear in the camera list. Connect your camera to the computer and then open the file.
	Opens your scanner software so you can scan a photo and have it appear in an Adobe PhotoDeluxe window. You must drag the scanner's plug-in module into the Acquire/Export folder in the Adobe PhotoDeluxe Plug-ins folder to have it appear in the scanner list. Choose your scanner from the list and then scan as usual.
	Opens a file stored on a Kodak Photo CD. You must have the PhotoCD in your drive to open a file. Double-click a photo to open it.

> If your camera or scanner doesn't have a plug-in that is compatible with Adobe PhotoDeluxe (or Adobe Photoshop™), save the digital photo or the scan as a TIFF or PICT file and store it on your hard disk.

If your copy center returns your scanned files on a floppy disk, copy the files to your hard disk and open them using the Open File button.

Saving photos

When you're working in On Your Own, Adobe PhotoDeluxe provides four basic choices for saving your photos. To save a photo, click Save/Print, click the Save tab, and then click one of the following buttons.

💾	Saves a photo as an Adobe PhotoDeluxe file. Saving a photo as an Adobe PhotoDeluxe file keeps all the layers. When you're working on a photo project, you should save frequently—at least every 15 minutes!
📁	Stores a photo in the Hold Photo folder. Use this button when you want to combine photos or parts of photos. See "Holding photos" and "Retrieving photos" on page 19 for more information about using this feature.
📄	Saves a photo as an Acrobat PDF file. Save a file in this format to send an electronic copy to someone who doesn't have Adobe PhotoDeluxe, or to someone who has a different computer type than you (Macintosh, Windows, DOS, or UNIX). The PDF file can be read using the Adobe Acrobat Reader, which comes with Adobe PhotoDeluxe.
🎞️	Saves a photo and puts it in a screen-saver slide show. You can play this slide show on your computer screen whenever you're not using your computer. The slide show is an After Dark module. A copy of the After Dark screen-saver/slide show module is included with Adobe PhotoDeluxe.

Exporting photos

File Format	Uses	Notes
Photoshop 3.0	Working with files in PhotoShop 3.0	This is the same file format as Adobe PhotoDeluxe. Saves layers.
Photoshop 2.0	Working with files in PhotoShop 2.0, 2.5, or applications that support only 2.0 or 2.5 files	Saves the file in Photoshop 2.0 format. Merges layers.
Adobe Acrobat	Sending files to others who don't have Adobe PhotoDeluxe or publishing on the Web	Saves the file in PDF format. Has the same effect as clicking Save/Print>Save>Create Acrobat File.
BMP	Saving files to be used on DOS and MS/Windows-compatible computers	In the dialog box, select Microsoft Windows or OS/2 format and indicate a bit depth.
EPS	Including files in an illustration or page-layout program such as Adobe Illustrator or Adobe PageMaker	See "Exporting in EPS format" on page 229 for information on setting EPS options.
JPEG	Compressing files	See "Exporting in JPEG format" on page 229 for information on setting JPEG options.
PCX	Saving files to be used on DOS and MS/Windows-compatible computers	
PICT File	Including files in Macintosh graphics and page-layout applications or as an intermediary file format for transferring files between applications	PICT format is especially effective for compressing images that contain large, flat areas of color.
PICT Resource	Using the file as a startup screen or including the file as a PICT resource in an application program	
Targa	Using files on systems that use the Truevision video board (supported by some MS-DOS color applications)	In the dialog box, select a resolution (in bit depth).
TIFF	Transferring files between applications and computer types	In the dialog box, select the Macintosh or Windows format. To compress as you save, click LZW compression.

Choosing file formats

To use a photo in	Save the photo as
Word-processing programs	TIFF PICT (Macintosh) BMP (Windows) PCX (Windows)
Page-layout programs	EPS TIFF
Illustration or drawing programs	EPS TIFF PICT BMP (Windows) PCX (Windows)

Printing photos

You can print Adobe PhotoDeluxe photos on your own printer, or you can take your photos to a copy center to have them printed. Adobe PhotoDeluxe provides three printing choices. To print a photo, click Save/Print, click the Print tab, and then click one of the following buttons.

Displays the Page Setup dialog box. These are the standard preview options that you get for all your applications. Select the options you want for printing the photo.

Displays a preview of the photo, showing its placement on the page and any borders you may placed have around the photo.

Displays the Print dialog box. Enter the number of copies you want to print. You can print a selection or the entire photo. Only visible layers are printed.

Ten Golden Rules of Using Adobe PhotoDeluxe

1 Have Fun! and save often.

2 Only one photo can be open at a time.

3 Select what you want to change.

4 Use small strokes when painting or editing.

5 Store selections on layers.

6 Smaller files are better.

7 You can only undo your last action (but you can choose File>Revert to Last Saved to get back to the last saved version of a photo).

8 Don't increase a photo's resolution in Adobe PhotoDeluxe.

9 There is no way to unmerge layers.

10 Archive your photos on custom CD-ROMs.